MISSOURI
COOK BOOK

Cooking Across America
Cookbook Collection™

**GOLDEN
WEST** ☼
PUBLISHERS

Front cover photo courtesy National Chicken Council, Washington, DC
Back cover photo of Gateway Arch courtesy Jefferson National Parks
Association, St. Louis, MO

Selected informational text from *Food in Missouri: A Cultural Stew:* The Curators of the University of Missouri, University of Missouri Press, Columbia

Printed in the United States of America

3rd Printing © 2004

ISBN #1-885590-60-1

Golden West Publishers, Inc.
4113 N. Longview Ave.
Phoenix, AZ 85014, USA
800-658-5830

For free sample recipes and complete Table of Contents for every Golden West cookbook, visit our website: **goldenwestpublishers.com**

Table of Contents

Appetizers & Beverages

Breakfasts & Brunches

Soups & Salads

Main Dishes

Table of Contents (Continued)

Side Dishes

Breads

Desserts

Introduction

From St. Louis to Kansas City, and Hannibal to Branson, Missouri blends a historic past with a multi-cultural present. As the gateway to the new frontier, Missouri towns were the stepping off posts for the Santa Fe and Oregon Trails. And today's Missouri serves as a base for exploring new wonders, with cosmopolitan cities such as St. Louis and Kansas City, emerging entertainment meccas like Branson, historical river towns at Cape Girardeau, Hannibal and St. Charles, and breathtaking scenery in the Ozarks and throughout the "show me" state.

Included among these wonders is the incredible variety of foods that help to define Missouri. The *Missouri Cook Book* presents a tasty array of Old World and modern-day delights. With wide ranging ethnic influences, Missouri's culinary heritage truly is a melting pot.

From *German Puff Pancakes* to *Missouri Sugar Cured Ham* and *Black Walnut Salad* to *Blueberry Buckle,* **Missouri Cook Book** will tempt your tastebuds while it teases your imagination. With recipes from homemakers, food manufacturers, farmers, restaurants and inns, this taste of Missouri will be a treasured keepsake and a great reminder of your time in Missouri!

Missouri Facts

Size—19th largest state with an area of 68,886 square miles
Population—5,595,211
State Capital—Jefferson City
Statehood—August 10, 1821, the 24th state admitted to the Union
State Nickname—The Show Me State
State Song—"Missouri Waltz" words by J. R. Shannon, music from
    John Valentine Eppel
State Motto—*Salus populi suprema lex esto*
    (The welfare of the people shall be
        the supreme law.)
State Bird—Bluebird
State Flower—Hawthorn
State Tree—Flowering Dogwood
State Animal—Mule
State Musical Instrument—Fiddle

State Insect
Honey Bee

State Folk Dance
Square Dance

Famous Missourians

Burt Bacharach, *songwriter;* **Josephine Baker,** *singer / human rights activist;* **Wallace Beery,** *actor;* **Thomas Benton,** *artist;* **Yogi Berra,** *baseball player;* **Omar Bradley,** *American general;* **Martha Jane Canary (Calamity Jane),** *frontierswoman;* **Dale Carnegie,** *teacher;* **George Washington Carver,** *scientist / inventor / educator;* **Samuel Clemens (Mark Twain),** *writer;* **Walter Cronkite,** *news correspondent;* **Robert Cummings,** *actor;* **Walt Disney,** *animation pioneer;* **T.S. Eliot,** *poet;* **James Fergason,** *inventor;* **Eugene Field,** *writer;* **Redd Foxx,** *actor / comedian;* **James Fulbright,** *politician;* **Richard Gephardt,** *politician;* **Betty Grable,** *actress;* **Joyce C. Hall,** *Hallmark Cards, Inc. founder;* **Jean Harlow,** *actress;* **John Huston,** *film director;* **Jesse James,** *outlaw;* **Scott Joplin,** *composer;* **Emmett Kelly,** *entertainer;* **William Lear,** *aviation inventor;* **Rush Limbaugh,** *radio / TV personality;* **Mary Margaret McBride,** *radio / TV personality;* **Stanley Frank Musial,** *baseball player;* **Geraldine Page,** *actress;* **James C. Penney,** *merchant;* **Marlin Perkins,** *zoologist;* **Vincent Price,** *actor;* **Ginger Rogers,** *dancer / actress;* **James Scott,** *ragtime musician / composer;* **Casey Stengel,** *baseball player / manager;* **Harry S. Truman,** *33rd president;* **Dick Van Dyke,** *actor;* **Dennis Weaver,** *actor.*

Missouri Visitor Information:
(573) 751-4133 or (800) 877-1234

Appetizers & Beverages

Party Cheese Ball

"This recipe was featured in our local newspaper. It is perfect to make and give as a Christmas gift."

Dortha J. Strack—Cape Girardeau

2 pkgs. (8 oz. ea.) CREAM CHEESE, softened
2 cups shredded SHARP CHEDDAR CHEESE
1 Tbsp. chopped PIMENTO
1 Tbsp. chopped GREEN BELL PEPPER
1 Tbsp. finely chopped ONION
2 tsp. WORCESTERSHIRE SAUCE
1 tsp. LEMON JUICE
Dash of CAYENNE
Dash of SALT
1/2 cup finely chopped PECANS

In a bowl, combine cream cheese and cheddar cheese; mix well. Add pimento, bell pepper, onion, Worcestershire sauce, lemon juice and seasonings; blend well. Chill mixture for 30 minutes, then shape into a ball and roll in pecans to coat.

Variations: Roll in finely chopped parsley or dried beef.

Sausage Balls

"This is a favorite during the holidays. I always have a Christmas Eve celebration and all of my family requests these."

Martha M. Darrough—Farmington

1 lb. GROUND PORK SAUSAGE
1 box (6 oz.) STOVE TOP® PORK
   STUFFING MIX
3/4 cup HOT WATER

1/2 cup chopped ONION
1/2 cup chopped CELERY
2 EGGS, well-beaten
1/2 tsp. BAKING POWDER

In a mixing bowl, combine sausage, stuffing mix and water. Add onion, celery, eggs and baking powder; mix well. Form into walnut-size balls and place on a broiler pan. Bake, covered, at 325° for 15 minutes or uncovered, at 350° for 25 minutes.

Did You Know?

The first successful parachute jump from a moving airplane was made in 1912 by Captain Albert Berry near St. Louis.

Shrimp, Onions & Capers

"This is a tangy variation on boiled shrimp and makes a delicious appetizer."

Thomas A. Tucker—Vivienne® Dressings/Tucker Food Products Inc., St. Louis

2 lbs. SHRIMP
1 med. WHITE ONION, thinly sliced
2 Tbsp. CAPERS, well-drained
1 bottle (8 oz.) VIVIENNE® ROMANO CHEESE DRESSING

Peel, devein and boil shrimp, using no seasoning in the boil; drain and place in a serving dish. Mix in onion and capers. Pour dressing over all ingredients and toss well. Serve immediately or serve chilled.

Serves 8-10.

Note: May be served over hot steamed rice as a main dish.

Vegetable Pancakes with Pesto Cream

"What a great way to eat your vegetables!
These tasty pancakes make a great hors d'ouvre!"

Cynthia Brogdon—The Doanleigh Inn, Kansas City

Batter:
   2 lg. POTATOES, shredded
   3 med. CARROTS, shredded
   1 med. ZUCCHINI, shredded
   3/4 cup chopped GREEN ONIONS
   1 tsp. SALT
   3/4 cup FLOUR
   3 EGGS, beaten
   1/4 tsp. PEPPER
   1 Tbsp. VEGETABLE OIL

Pesto Cream:
   1 cup SOUR CREAM
   2 Tbsp. BASIL PESTO

To prepare batter: Rinse and drain shredded potatoes; squeeze dry and place in a large bowl. Add carrots, zucchini, onions and salt. Let stand for 10-15 minutes or until vegetables release some liquid. Stir flour, eggs and pepper into vegetables. In a large skillet, heat oil. Pour 1/4 cup of batter for each pancake into skillet and flatten slightly with a spatula. Cook pancakes until golden brown and crispy on both sides. To prepare pesto cream: In a small bowl, stir sour cream and pesto together until smooth. Serve pancakes with pesto cream on the side.

Kansas City

The Kansa Indians were the first to live at the meeting place of the Kansas and Missouri rivers. In 1821, Francois Chouteau settled the area by establishing a trading post on the bluffs of the Missouri River. Today, Kansas City accommodates nearly 200 of the nation's largest industrial firms including auto assembly, steel and metal fabrication and food processing plants.

BG's Pizza

"This is a tasty creation for a different type of pizza."

Barbara Gray—Ballwin

1 (12-inch) BOBOLI® PIZZA CRUST
2 cloves GARLIC
1 med. ONION
3 oz. CREAM CHEESE, softened
1 ctn. (8 oz.) SOUR CREAM
3 tsp. ITALIAN SEASONING, divided
1 TOMATO, thinly sliced
1 cup grated CHEDDAR CHEESE
1 cup SALSA
1 can (6 oz.) BLACK OLIVES, drained and sliced

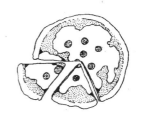

Precook pizza crust according to package directions; allow to cool. With the steel blade in the work bowl of a food processor, pulse garlic until fine, then add onion. Stir in cream cheese, sour cream and 2 teaspoons of Italian seasoning and mix thoroughly. Spread mixture on pizza crust; arrange tomato on top of mixture and sprinkle with cheddar cheese. Mix remaining Italian seasoning with salsa and spread over cheddar cheese; arrange olives on top. Cut into wedges and serve.

Golden Fried Onion Rings

Missouri Soybean Merchandising Council—Jefferson City

1/2 cup DEFATTED SOY FLOUR
1 1/2 cups ALL-PURPOSE FLOUR
1/4 Tbsp. CHICKEN BOUILLON
Dash of SEASONED SALT
1/4 tsp. ONION SALT
1/2 tsp. ACCENT®
1 tsp. SUGAR

3/4 tsp. SALT
1 cup 2% LOW FAT MILK
1 cup COLD WATER
1 lg. EGG
1 lg. VIDALIA ONION, cut to
    1/2-inch slices
SOY OIL for frying

In a bowl, combine dry ingredients and mix well with wire whisk; set aside. In another bowl, combine milk, water and egg and beat with electric mixer. Combine wet and dry ingredients and beat until batter is smooth. Heat soy oil in deep-fat fryer to 375°. Using a fork, dip onion rings into batter and carefully place in hot oil. Fry for 2-3 minutes or until golden brown.

Hot Wings

"Who says Missouri doesn't like it hot? Great Grandma used to eat hot chile peppers straight without even a dare! We grow a variety of our own organic chile peppers to make A Taste of the Kingdom® pepper jellies that offer different levels of heat to suit everyone!"

Julie Jones Price—A Taste of the Kingdom, LLC, Kingdom City

2 lbs. CHICKEN WINGS
A TASTE OF THE KINGDOM® PEPPER JELLY

Prepare grill for cooking. When coals are ready, place wings on grill over hot coals but not directly over flames. Cook for 45 minutes. Brush wings generously with pepper jelly and cook for an additional 15 minutes or until glaze has formed. Do not use barbecue sauce on wings.

Note: Heat pepper jelly in microwave for smoother spreading.

Hannibal

This northeastern Missouri city was the boyhood home of Samuel Clemens (Mark Twain) and was depicted in his novels "The Adventures of Huckleberry Finn" and "The Adventures of Tom Sawyer."

Soft Goat Cheese

Use this in dips, cheese balls and cheesecakes. Spread on crackers or crumble on top of spaghetti sauce.

Goats-R-Us—United Missouri Goat Producers, Salem

1 gal. PASTEURIZED GOAT'S　　**1/4 tsp. RENNET**
**　MILK, room temperature**　　**1/4 cup COLD WATER**
1/2 cup BUTTERMILK

In a large bowl, combine goat milk and buttermilk. In a small bowl, dissolve rennet in water; add to milk mixture. Let set until clabbered (thickened), then pour into a colander lined with cheesecloth. Allow to drain well. Cheese can be kept in the refrigerator for a couple of days or frozen for later use.

Ostrich Wraps

Ostrich meat is a satisfying alternative for red-meat lovers. The color, flavor and texture is similar to beef with two-thirds less fat.

Greater Missouri Ostrich Association—Hermitage

Prepared BREAD DOUGH
1 lb. GROUND OSTRICH, cooked
2 1/2 cups MOZZARELLA CHEESE
1 1/2 cups SPAGHETTI SAUCE
1 1/4 tsp. ITALIAN SEASONING
1/4 tsp. CHILI POWDER
1/2 tsp. GARLIC POWDER
SALT and PEPPER
1 EGG
1/4 cup SESAME SEEDS

Roll bread dough out fairly thin and cut into 4-inch squares. In a large bowl, combine remaining ingredients, except for egg and sesame seeds and mix well. Place large spoonfuls of meat mixture in the center of each square. Pull opposite corners up, pinch edges together to seal and twist the very top. In a small bowl, beat the egg lightly, then brush on top of wraps. Sprinkle wraps with sesame seeds and place on a greased baking sheet; let rise. Bake at 375° for 20 minutes.

Makes 10-12 wraps.

Soybeans In Missouri

More soybeans are grown in the U.S. than anywhere else in the world and they are the number one cash crop in Missouri. Rich in protein and a natural source of dietary fiber, soybeans contain iron, B-vitamins, calcium and zinc along with eight essential amino acids. They have also proven effective in lowering cholesterol levels.

Soybean Cheese Balls

Missouri Soybean Merchandising Council—Jefferson City

1 sm. ONION, minced
2 Tbsp. OIL
1 cup SOYBEAN CHEESE
1 cup BREAD CRUMBS
1/4 cup MILK
2 Tbsp. chopped NUTS
SAGE

In a skillet, sauté onion in oil until translucent. Add cheese, bread crumbs milk and nuts; blend well. Season with sage to taste. Form mixture into balls and place on a cookie sheet. Bake at 350° for 12 minutes or until brown.

Hush Puppies

Though the exact origin is unknown, the hush puppy is thought to have emerged sometime in the 1800's. One theory holds that after a long day of fishing and hunting, hunters would gather around the campfire to fry up their catch. To silence their whining hunting dogs, they would throw them bits of the fried corn batter and hence, hush puppies were born.

1 cup WHITE CORNMEAL
1 1/2 tsp. FLOUR
1/2 tsp. BAKING POWDER
1 tsp. SUGAR
3/4 tsp. SALT

1/2 cup BUTTERMILK
1 EGG, beaten
1/2 sm. ONION, finely
**   minced**
1 qt. VEGETABLE OIL

In a large bowl, sift together dry ingredients. In a separate bowl, combine buttermilk, egg and onion; pour into dry ingredients. Mix well but do not overbeat. In a deep-fat fryer, heat oil to 375°. Drop batter by tablespoons into hot oil. Cook hush puppies for 3 minutes or until they turn golden brown and float to the top. Remove with a slotted spoon and drain on paper towels.

Makes 12 hush puppies.

Bottoms Up!
Anheuser-Busch brewery in St. Louis is the largest beer producing plant in the nation.

Coffee Banana Smoothie

"Kansas City loves coffee! This smoothie is a standard at The Supreme Bean coffee house."

Cynthia Brogdon—The Supreme Bean, Kansas City

2 BANANAS, peeled and frozen
1 1/2 cups SKIM MILK
8 oz. VANILLA YOGURT

1/4 tsp. CINNAMON
2 shots (1-1 1/2 oz. ea.)
ESPRESSO

In a blender, combine all ingredients and blend until smooth. If desired, garnish with fresh bananas and mint.

Soy Shakes

Note: For colder, thicker shakes, use partially frozen soy milk!

Double Citrus Soy Shake

1 (2 1/2 oz.) CITRUS FRUIT JUICE BAR
1/2 cup chilled SOY MILK
1 Tbsp. FROZEN ORANGE JUICE CONCENTRATE
1 Tbsp. SUGAR
1/4 tsp. VANILLA

Allow citrus bar to thaw slightly. Break bar into pieces and place in blender. Add other ingredients and blend at low speed for 10 seconds.

Serves 1.

Butterscotch Soy Shake

1/2 cup chilled SOY MILK
1/4 tsp. VANILLA
2 Tbsp. MILK-FREE BUTTERSCOTCH SAUCE

Place all ingredients in a blender and blend at low speed for about 10 seconds.

Peanut Butter-Honey Soy Shake

1/2 cup chilled SOY MILK
1/4 cup SOY FORMULA or NONDAIRY CREAMER
2 Tbsp. SMOOTH PEANUT BUTTER
1 Tbsp. HONEY
1/4 tsp. VANILLA

Place all ingredients in a blender and blend at low speed for about 10 seconds or until smooth.

Breakfasts & Brunches

Sweetbriar
Baked Eggs & Mushrooms

"A friend gave us this recipe. This is the most requested recipe by our guests. Curry powder gives this dish a special flavor and is complemented with bacon or sausage."

Carolyn & George Sweet—Sweetbriar Bed & Breakfast, Fayette

5 Tbsp. BUTTER, divided
2 cups fresh MUSHROOMS, halved
1 Tbsp. finely chopped ONION
3 Tbsp. FLOUR
1 1/2 cups MILK, heated
1 tsp. CHICKEN STOCK POWDER
1/2 tsp. CURRY POWDER
1/4 tsp. SALT
1/4 tsp. PEPPER
6 HARD-BOILED EGGS, quartered
1/2 cup BUTTERED BREAD CRUMBS
1 Tbsp. PARSLEY FLAKES

Preheat oven to 350°. In a saucepan, melt 2 tablespoons of butter and sauté mushrooms and onion for 5 minutes or until mushrooms begin to brown. In a large skillet, melt remaining butter, add flour and cook over medium heat until mixture bubbles. Stir in milk, chicken stock powder, curry powder, salt and pepper and cook for 2 minutes over low heat. Remove from heat; set aside. Arrange eggs, yolk-side up in a buttered shallow baking dish. Combine mushroom mixture with milk mixture, pour over eggs and sprinkle with bread crumbs and parsley. Bake for 40 minutes until top is golden brown.

Appel Pannekoek

(Apple Pancake)

"This is a specialty breakfast that we serve to our guests."

Kay Cameron—Cameron's Crag Bed & Breakfast, Branson

1 tsp. CINNAMON
1 Tbsp. SUGAR
1 lg. APPLE, peeled and sliced
1 Tbsp. BUTTER
3 EGGS

1/2 cup FLOUR
1/2 cup MILK
1/8 tsp. NUTMEG
1/4 tsp. VANILLA

Preheat oven to 425°. In a small dish, mix cinnamon and sugar together; sprinkle mixture over apple. Melt butter in a baking dish or skillet. Spread apples over melted butter and place in oven until very hot. In a mixing bowl, combine eggs, flour, milk, nutmeg and vanilla; mix well. Add batter to hot apple mixture and bake for 15 minutes or until lightly browned.

Serves 2.

Lococo House II French Toast

"I wanted a signature breakfast item for my Bed & Breakfast, so I developed this recipe."

Rhona Lococo—Lococo House II Bed & Breakfast, St. Charles

3 EGGS
1 3/4 cups HALF AND HALF
1 Tbsp. ORANGE JUICE
   CONCENTRATE
1/4 cup SUGAR

1 tsp. VANILLA
6 slices FRENCH BREAD
SHREDDED COCONUT
BROWN SUGAR
3 tsp. MARGARINE

Mix the first five ingredients in a blender. Dip bread into mixture and arrange in a generously greased 9-inch deep dish pie pan. Pour remaining mixture over bread and allow to set for 30 minutes. Sprinkle with coconut and brown sugar to taste, then dot top with margarine. Bake at 350° for 30 minutes.

Note: Flavoring of choice may be added to egg mixture.

 Breakfasts & Brunches

German Puff Pancake with Cinnamon Apple Topping

"Our guests love this breakfast treat."

Kay Cameron—Cameron's Crag Bed & Breakfast, Branson

2 Tbsp. BUTTER	**1/2 cup FLOUR**
3 EGGS	**1/2 cup MILK**

Melt butter in a glass baking dish. In a bowl, beat eggs, flour and milk together. Pour into baking dish and bake at 425° for 15 minutes or until nicely browned. Serve **Cinnamon Apple Topping** over pancake.

Cinnamon Apple Topping

1 tsp. CINNAMON	**2 lg. APPLES, peeled and diced**
1 Tbsp. SUGAR	**3/4 cup PANCAKE SYRUP**

In a small bowl, combine cinnamon and sugar together. Place apples in a microwaveable bowl and sprinkle with cinnamon mixture; stir to coat well. Pour syrup over apple mixture and microwave until apples are tender.

Sautéed Pears

"This recipe makes wonderful use of pears and is a tasty addition to your breakfast menu."

Lori and Dean Murray—Eastlake Inn Bed & Breakfast, St. Louis

Quarter, core and slice **PEARS.** In a saucepan, sauté pears in **BUTTER** over medium heat until tender and lightly browned. Make sure to use enough butter so pan does not dry out. Add **BROWN SUGAR** to pears as desired and stir until well-coated. Place in fruit cups and top with a dollop of **WHIPPED CREAM.**

Apple Strudel Waffles with Apple Cider Syrup

"These delicious waffles and syrup taste just like grandma's homemade apple strudel. Our guests can't get enough of them!"

Lawrence A. Stevens—The Dickey House Bed & Breakfast Ltd.,
Marshfield

3 med. GRANNY SMITH APPLES
1 Tbsp. BROWN SUGAR
2 cups BISQUICK® MIX (or your favorite dry waffle mix)
1 lg. EGG, beaten
1/2 tsp. grated ORANGE PEEL
1/2 tsp. grated LEMON PEEL
1 tsp. PURE VANILLA EXTRACT
(do not use imitation)
3/4 tsp. CINNAMON
3/4 - 1 cup MILK or CLUB SODA*
1/4 cup RAISINS
1/3 cup chopped WALNUTS
WHIPPED CREAM

Preheat Belgian waffle iron. Peel, core and thinly slice apples; place in a microwavable glass bowl. Sprinkle with brown sugar and toss lightly. Microwave, uncovered, on High for 2 minutes; set aside. In a large bowl, mix all remaining ingredients except for raisins, walnuts and whipped cream. When the batter is smooth, stir in raisins and walnuts; allow to stand for 5 minutes. Stir batter and pour 1/4-1/3 cup of the batter onto waffle iron. Arrange apple slices on each waffle; close the iron and cook until golden brown. Arrange waffles on top of each other, slightly offset. Top with whipped cream and remaining apple slices. Serve with ***Apple Cider Syrup.***

* Whole milk makes the waffles heavier and they will bake to a rich dark brown color. Club soda makes the waffles very light and they will bake to a beautiful golden brown.

(Continued next page)

Apple Strudel Waffles with Apple Cider Syrup
(Continued from previous page)

Apple Cider Syrup

2 Tbsp. BUTTER
1/4 cup packed BROWN SUGAR
1 cup APPLE CIDER or APPLE JUICE
1/2 tsp. CINNAMON

In a medium saucepan, combine all ingredients and bring to a boil. Reduce heat and simmer for 10 minutes or until thick and smooth, stirring frequently to prevent scorching.

Note: Add 1/2 teaspoon of cornstarch to the mixture if you are in a hurry and wish to thicken it quickly.

Did You Know?
Ballwin is unique! It is the only city in America with this name!

Mexican Breakfast Delight

"This is a recipe I use for the Men's Fellowship Breakfast as well as other brunch events at our church."

Robert A. Gray—Ballwin

2 Tbsp. OIL
1 1/2 cups frozen HASHBROWNS
1/2 cup chopped ONION
1/4 cup chopped RED BELL PEPPER
1/4 cup chopped GREEN BELL PEPPER
1/2 cup chopped HAM
3/4 cup shredded CHEDDAR CHEESE
3 EGGS, beaten
SALT and PEPPER
1/4 cup chopped BLACK OLIVES

In a large skillet, heat oil and brown hashbrowns. Add onion and bell pepper and sauté until tender. Add ham and heat thoroughly. In a bowl, combine cheese and eggs, then stir into ham mixture. Sauté, stirring constantly, until eggs are cooked but still moist; season with salt and pepper to taste. Transfer to plates, sprinkle with additional cheese; top with olives.

Serves 2.

★ ★ ★ ★ *Cooking Across America* ★ ★ ★ ★

Kansas City Scramble

"This delicious variation on scrambled eggs is a favorite at The Doanleigh Inn, Kansas City's first Bed & Breakfast."

Cynthia Brogdon—The Doanleigh Inn, Kansas City

1-2 Tbsp. OLIVE OIL	**2 cups shredded CHEDDAR**
4 cups diced POTATOES	**CHEESE**
12 EGGS	**PARSLEY SPRIGS for garnish**

In a skillet, heat oil, add potatoes and cook for 15-20 minutes, stirring occasionally. In a bowl, whisk eggs and add to potatoes. Cook for 4-5 minutes or until slightly set. Stir in cheese and 1 cup of **Ranch Dressing**. Cook for 8-10 minutes or until set. Garnish with parsley and serve with an English muffin.

Serves 4.

Ranch Dressing

1 Tbsp. ONION FLAKES	**1/8 tsp. PEPPER**
1/4 tsp. BASIL	**1/2 tsp. SALT**
1/4 tsp. THYME	**1/2 cup YOGURT**
1/4 tsp. GARLIC POWDER	**1/2 cup MAYONNAISE**
1 Tbsp. PARSLEY FLAKES	**16 oz. BUTTERMILK**

Mix dry ingredients well, then add yogurt, mayonnaise and buttermilk; mix thoroughly. Dressing can be stored in an airtight container in refrigerator for up to one week.

George Washington Carver National Monument

Located in Diamond, near Joplin, this monument preserves the birthplace of George Washington Carver. Born as a slave and then raised by farmers Moses and Susan Carver, he distinguished himself in the field of botany and the teaching of scientific agriculture. He developed more than 300 peanut byproducts, including instant coffee, over 100 sweet potato byproducts and discovered new uses for soybeans, cowpeas and other crops. In 1945, Congress designated January 5th as George Washington Carver Day.

Pumpkin French Toast

"As an Innkeeper, I am always looking for different recipes. French toast of some variety is always served with breakfast at our B & B. I wanted a toast that said 'autumn,' so I experimented a bit. My Pumpkin French Toast fills the bill!"

Jane Due—Ray Home Bed & Breakfast, Gallatin

6 slices FRENCH BREAD, 1 1/2-inches thick

Filling:
   1 cup canned PUMPKIN
   1 tsp. CINNAMON
   1/2 tsp. NUTMEG
   1 tsp. SUGAR

Egg Mixture:
   6 EGGS
   1 1/2 cups EVAPORATED MILK
   1 tsp. NUTMEG
   1 tsp. VANILLA
   1/3 cup SUGAR

3 Tbsp. SHORTENING

Preheat oven to 350°. Cut a "pocket" in each slice of bread. In a bowl, combine filling ingredients and mix well. Stuff bread "pockets" with filling mixture and place in a glass baking dish. In another bowl, beat egg mixture ingredients together; pour over bread and allow to soak for at least one hour in refrigerator. In a heavy skillet, heat shortening and lightly brown bread slices. Place bread in a 13 x 9 dish and bake, covered, for 30-45 minutes. Serve with maple syrup.

Serves 6.

Breakfast Anyone?

Aunt Jemima® pancake flour was invented in St. Joseph in 1889 and was the first ready-mix food ever to be introduced commercially.

Lemon Ricotta Pancakes

"This is my new recipe for very light and fragrant pancakes!"

Cathy McGeorge—Loganberry Inn Bed & Breakfast, Fulton

1 1/3 cups RICOTTA CHEESE
3 EGGS, lightly beaten
3 Tbsp. SUGAR
2 tsp. LEMON JUICE
1 Tbsp. grated LEMON PEEL
2 Tbsp. BUTTER, melted
1/2 cup MILK

1 cup FLOUR
1 tsp. BAKING POWDER
Dash of SALT
Fresh BLACKBERRIES for
    garnish
POWDERED SUGAR
LEMON ZEST

Preheat griddle to 325°. In a bowl, combine cheese, eggs, sugar, lemon juice, lemon peel, butter and milk; mix until smooth. Add flour, baking powder and salt; stir until just blended. Pour 1/4 cup of mixture onto lightly greased griddle and cook until lightly browned on both sides. Stack pancakes on a plate and surround with blackberries; dust with powdered sugar and accent with lemon zest.

Makes 12 pancakes.

Milk Toast

"We had our own cow when I was a child and we ate this dish for breakfast as kids eat cereal today. We had homemade bread then, so the taste will be different now with store-bought bread. This dish is especially good on a cold morning and a good way to use up leftover pieces of bread."

Betty Glastetter—Oran

BUTTER
2 slices TOAST
1 1/2 cups HOT MILK

CINNAMON
SUGAR

Butter slices of toast. Cut into small pieces and place in a bowl. Add milk and cinnamon and sugar to taste.

Serves 1.

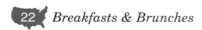

Company French Toast

"This recipe originated in the Shepherdsfield kitchen, located in Callaway County, which has been producing hundreds of meals weekly since 1979. It is especially popular because you can make it ahead. It is also delicious made with Shepherdsfield Bakery's Cinnamon-Raisin Bread."

Debbie Mahaney—Shepherdsfield Country Store & Bakery, Fulton

1/2 cup MARGARINE
1/2 cup PANCAKE SYRUP
1 tsp. CINNAMON
12 slices SHEPHERDSFIELD® WHOLE-WHEAT BREAD
    or CINNAMON-RAISIN BREAD
6 EGGS
1 1/2 cups MILK
Pinch of SALT

Melt margarine in a 13 x 9 baking dish. Add pancake syrup and sprinkle cinnamon on top; cover with bread slices. In a bowl, beat eggs; stir in milk and salt. Pour mixture over bread; cover and refrigerate overnight. Bake, uncovered, at 350° for 45 minutes. Cut into squares and serve hot with syrup.

Serves 8-10.

The Pony Express

On April 3, 1860, horseback riders began carrying mail between St. Joseph, MO and Sacramento, CA, following the well-known Oregon-California Trail. This saved over 100 miles over the longer southern route used by stagecoaches of the Butterfield Overland Mail. Young riders rode at top speed between relay stations that stood 10-15 miles apart and earned $100-$150 a month. The Pony Express ended on October 24, 1861 due to the coast-to-coast communication offered by the telegraph.

Baked French Toast

Camden County Historical Society—Linn Creek

1 loaf FRENCH BREAD, cut into 8 slices
5 EGGS, beaten
1/4 tsp. BAKING POWDER
3/4 cup MILK
1 Tbsp. VANILLA
1 pkg. (16 oz.) frozen STRAWBERRIES
1 Tbsp. APPLE PIE SPICE
4 BANANAS, sliced
1 cup SUGAR
CINNAMON-SUGAR MIXTURE

   Place bread in a large baking dish. Combine eggs, baking powder, milk and vanilla. Pour mixture over bread, cover and refrigerate overnight. In a separate large baking dish, combine strawberries, apple pie spice, bananas and sugar. Layer bread slices over fruit; sprinkle with cinnamon-sugar mixture. Bake at 425° for 20-25 minutes.

The Camden County Museum

The Camden County Historical Society Museum features vintage working looms and has woven rugs available for sale as well as historical journals and locally handcrafted items in its gift shop. Historical research is available, by appointment.

Tomato Omelet

Camden County Historical Society—Linn Creek

4 EGGS, separated   1/4 cup TOMATO JUICE
1/2-1 tsp. SALT   1/2 Tbsp. BUTTER, melted
1/8 tsp. PEPPER

   In a small mixing bowl, beat egg yolks until thick and lemon colored; add salt and pepper. In a separate bowl, beat egg whites until foamy; add tomato juice and resume beating until stiff. Carefully fold into egg yolks. In a cast-iron skillet, heat butter and pour in egg mixture. Cook over low heat until puffed up. Place in oven and bake at 325° until firm. Fold and serve.

Soups & Salads

Vegetable Soup

"To call this vegetable soup belies its truly unique and hearty flavor. Consider three slightly unusual ingredients: sweet potatoes, celery seed and cumin. Amounts of the latter two can be adjusted to suit your taste as you make this your own dish. It's become a favorite of ours and of our guests."

Kathy & Tom Corey—Rock Eddy Bluff Farm–A Country Retreat, Dixon

1/4 cup BUTTER or MARGARINE	2 med. POTATOES,
1 lg. ONION, chopped	peeled and shredded
3 med. SWEET POTATOES,	2 tsp. CELERY SEED
peeled and chopped	2 tsp. CUMIN
3 med. ZUCCHINI, chopped	1 tsp. PEPPER
1 bunch BROCCOLI, chopped	2 cups LIGHT CREAM
2 qts. CHICKEN BROTH	

In a large kettle, melt butter and sauté onion until translucent. Add sweet potatoes, zucchini and broccoli. Sauté for 5 minutes, then stir in broth and simmer for 5 minutes. Add potatoes and seasonings and cook for an additional 10 minutes until vegetables are tender. Stir in cream and heat through.

Serves 12-16.

Crockpot Bean Soup

"This is a great crockpot soup. I came up with it by adding vegetables to tomato soup. It is very tasty."

Georgia L. Snider—Chaffee

1 lb. GREAT NORTHERN BEANS
1 lb. SMOKED HAM, diced
1 cup sliced CELERY
1 cup chopped ONION
1 cup chopped CARROTS
2 BAY LEAVES
1 can (14.5 oz.) STEWED TOMATOES
2 cans (10.75 oz.) TOMATO SOUP
SALT and PEPPER
1 Tbsp. CHILI POWDER

Soak beans overnight in 6 cups of water; drain. Place beans in a crockpot and add water to cover. Stir in remaining ingredients. Cover and cook on high for 3 hours, then turn to low and cook for 10-14 hours. Remove bay leaves. Serve with cornbread on the side.

Milk Soup

"I was raised on a small farm and we had our own cows to milk each day. This was a quick and easy dish to make."

Betty Glastetter—Oran

1 qt. MILK
1/2 cup FLOUR
1 EGG, beaten

4 Tbsp. SUGAR
Dash of CINNAMON

In a saucepan, scald milk. In a bowl, combine flour and egg; do not stir, but "fork" until it takes up the flour. The mixture should be in small crumbles or pieces. Add sugar to milk, then slowly add egg mixture while stirring. Cook for 2-3 minutes; do not boil. Sprinkle with cinnamon when ready to serve.

Note: Soup can be refrigerated, but it will be thicker the next day. Reheat in the microwave for 1-2 minutes.

Super 16-Bean Soup

"The longer you simmer this soup, the better it gets. It is best served with Shepherdsfield Bakery's sour dough bread."

Debbie Mahaney—Shepherdsfield Country Store & Bakery, Fulton

1 1/2 cups 16-BEAN MIX	1/2 cup TOMATO SAUCE or
6 cups BOILING WATER	TOMATO PURÉE
1/4 lb. BACON	4 cups BEEF STOCK
1 cup chopped ONION	1 Tbsp. SALT
1 cup chopped CELERY	1/2 tsp. PEPPER
1/2 clove GARLIC, minced	2 cubes CHICKEN BOUILLON
1 cup diced CARROTS	2 Tbsp. RED WINE VINEGAR
2 cups diced POTATOES	2 cups diced GARLIC SAUSAGE
2 BAY LEAVES	1 cup sliced LEEKS, optional

Rinse and pick over beans. Carefully pour beans into boiling water; turn off heat and soak for 1/2 hour. In a small skillet, sauté bacon; add onion, celery and garlic and cook until onion is translucent. In a soup kettle, combine beans with water, bacon mixture and remaining ingredients, except for red wine vinegar, sausage and leeks. Cover and simmer for 1 1/2 hours. Add vinegar and adjust salt and pepper accordingly. Add water or broth to thin soup if necessary. Stir in sausage and leeks. Heat thoroughly and serve.

Note: Substitute dried lentils for beans if desired.

Serves 6-8.

Cape Girardeau

This bustling riverside city was named after Jean Baptiste Girardot whose trading post was established in 1733 at Cape Rock, just 2 miles northeast. Cape Girardeau is home to Southeast Missouri State University, Trail of Tears State Park and the Cape River Heritage Museum. It is also the hometown of radio personality Rush Limbaugh.

Pumpkin Soup

2 1/2 cups cooked PUMPKIN
1 1/2 cups WATER
3 cups MILK
1/3 cup cooked RICE
2 Tbsp. BUTTER
1 tsp. chopped PARSLEY
VEGETABLE SALT

In a saucepan, combine pumpkin with water. Bring almost to boiling point; add milk and reheat. Place pumpkin mixture and remaining ingredients in a double boiler, seasoning with vegetable salt to taste. Cover and cook for 15 minutes.

Corn Chowder

"This recipe comes from my son and his wife who are both graduates of the Culinary Institute of America."

Robert A. Gray—Ballwin

1 cup diced uncooked BACON
1 ONION, finely chopped
4 cloves GARLIC, minced
1 pkg. (16 oz.) frozen CORN
1 can (15 oz.) CREAM STYLE
   CORN
1 gal. CHICKEN STOCK

4 POTATOES, diced

Roux:
   1 cup FLOUR
   1 cup UNSALTED
     BUTTER, melted

SALT and PEPPER

In a large skillet, sauté bacon until lightly crisp, add onion and sauté for 5 minutes. Add garlic and sauté for an additional 5 minutes. Stir in corn, cream style corn and chicken stock and simmer for 20 minutes. Add potatoes and cook for 15 minutes or until tender. Remove solids and set aside. To prepare roux: Mix flour and butter in a 4-cup glass measuring cup. Microwave on High for 4-5 minutes, stirring often towards the end. Be careful as this is very hot. Whisk roux into soup, a small amount at a time, to thicken. Season with salt and pepper to taste. Return solids back to soup and stir gently.

Makes 1 gallon.

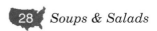

Veggie-Ham Chowder

"I like to cook in the microwave, so I took a simple chowder recipe and developed this version that everybody really enjoys."

Barbara Gray—Ballwin

2 cups diced CAULIFLOWER
1 sm. ONION, chopped
2 cloves GARLIC, minced
1 can (14.5 oz.) LOW SODIUM CHICKEN BROTH
1 cup MILK or LIGHT CREAM
1 can (10.75 oz.) CREAM OF POTATO
    SOUP
2 Tbsp. CORNSTARCH
1/4 cup COLD WATER
1/4 tsp. WHITE PEPPER
1 can (15 oz.) CREAM STYLE CORN
2 cups finely diced cooked HAM
GREEN ONIONS with tops for garnish

Place cauliflower, onion, garlic and broth in a 3-quart casserole dish. Cover and microwave on High for 3-5 minutes until tender; do not drain. In a medium bowl, combine milk and soup and blend well. Stir cornstarch into water and slowly add to soup mixture. Stir soup mixture into the cauliflower mixture; add pepper and corn and blend well. Microwave on High for 2-3 minutes until thick and heated through. Stir in ham. Microwave on High for 1 minute. Garnish with green onions.

Serves 6-8.

The "Spirit of St. Louis"

In 1927, Charles Augustus Lindbergh persuaded nine St. Louis businessmen to help him finance the "Spirit of St. Louis." Lindbergh tested the plane with a flight from New York to San Diego, setting a transcontinental record. On May 20, 1927 Lindbergh took off from New York and flew over 3,600 miles in 33.5 hours to Paris, completing the first solo nonstop flight across the Atlantic Ocean on May 21st.

Salmon Chowder

"This tasty chowder contains the 'Holy Trinity' (onions, peppers and celery), ingredients that serve well in most soups, chowders and stews."

Kathy & Tom Corey—Rock Eddy Bluff Farm–A Country Retreat, Dixon

1/4 cup OIL
1 sm. ONION, finely
   chopped
1/2 cup diced CELERY
1/4 cup diced GREEN BELL
   PEPPER
2-3 sm. POTATOES, chopped
1 cup WATER

1 can (14.75 oz.) RED or PINK
   SALMON, do not drain
1 cup MILK
1 cup CREAM
2 Tbsp. BUTTER
GARLIC or GARLIC POWDER
PAPRIKA

In a large saucepan, heat oil and sauté onion, celery and bell pepper until onion is translucent. Add potatoes and water and cook until potatoes are tender. Shred salmon with a fork and stir into soup. Stir in milk and cream. Simmer for 1 hour; do not boil. Add butter and stir until melted. Season with garlic to taste. Sprinkle with paprika for added color.

Spinach Salad

1 lb. fresh SPINACH
4 ORANGES, peeled
   and chunked
1 med. ONION, sliced into rings

1 clove GARLIC, minced
3 HARD-BOILED EGGS, sliced
4 slices BACON, cooked
   and crumbled

Wash, dry and remove stems from spinach. In a salad bowl, toss spinach, oranges, onion and garlic; refrigerate. Mix in eggs, bacon and *Orange Dressing* just before serving.

Orange Dressing

3 Tbsp. ORANGE JUICE
   CONCENTRATE
1 Tbsp. LIME JUICE
2 Tbsp. RICE WINE VINEGAR

2 Tbsp. HONEY
1 tsp. DIJON MUSTARD
1 Tbsp. toasted slivered
   ALMONDS

Combine all dressing ingredients and refrigerate.

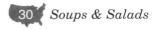

The Original Bogey Club & Frontier Room Salad

"A classic dish that originated in 1948 at this famous St. Louis country club and was later featured at the legendary Frontier Room Restaurant."

Thomas A. Tucker—Vivienne® Dressings/Tucker Food Products Inc., St. Louis

1 head ROMAINE LETTUCE
1 head ICEBERG LETTUCE
1/4 cup sliced RADISHES
1/4 cup chopped GREEN ONIONS
1 bottle (8 oz.) VIVIENNE® ROMANO
    CHEESE DRESSING
Julienne SWISS CHEESE for garnish

Thoroughly rinse lettuce, dry and tear into bite-size pieces. In a large salad bowl, combine all ingredients; toss well. Serve chilled. Garnish with Swiss cheese. Add sliced, poached chicken breast for a complete entrée.

Serves 6-8.

 # Pretzel Salad

Missouri Small Fruit Growers Association—Neosho

2 1/2 cups PRETZELS, crushed
3/4 cup BUTTER, melted
1 cup + 3 Tbsp. SUGAR, divided
1 pkg. (8 oz.) CREAM CHEESE,
    softened

2 cups COOL WHIP®
2 pkgs. (6 oz. ea.)
    STRAWBERRY JELL-O®
4 cups BOILING WATER
Frozen STRAWBERRIES

In a small bowl, mix pretzels, butter and 3 tablespoons of sugar together. Press mixture into a 13 x 9 baking pan. Bake at 375° for 13 minutes; cool. In a small bowl, mix cream cheese, remaining sugar and Cool Whip together and spread over pretzel mixture. Refrigerate for 4-6 hours. In a bowl, dissolve Jell-O in boiling water. Add frozen strawberries to taste. Allow to cool for 30 minutes, then pour over cream cheese mixture. Chill for 2 hours before serving.

Peachtree Pork Salad

Missouri Pork Producers Association—Columbia

1 jar (10 oz.) PEACH PRESERVES
1/4 cup WHITE WINE VINEGAR
2 Tbsp. DIJON MUSTARD
1 (2 lb.) PORK TENDERLOIN
1 pkg. (10 oz.) MIXED SALAD GREENS
2 cups fresh or frozen (thawed) PEACH SLICES or
 1 can (16 oz.) sliced PEACHES, drained
1 cup fresh or frozen (slightly thawed)
 RASPBERRIES
1 sm. RED ONION, cut into 1/8-inch slices
 and separated into rings
1/2 cup ALFALFA SPROUTS

In a small bowl, combine preserves, vinegar and mustard. Cut pork tenderloin in half lengthwise, cutting to, but not through, the bottom; open and flatten. Brush both sides of tenderloin with 1/3 cup of preserve mixture. Place meat on a broiler pan and broil 4-6 inches from heat for 5-6 minutes. Turn, brush with 2 tablespoons of the preserve mixture and broil for an additional 7 minutes. Arrange salad greens on four salad plates. Cut tenderloin into 1/2-inch thick slices and place in center of greens. Arrange peaches, raspberries, onion and alfalfa sprouts around meat. Drizzle with remaining peach preserve mixture.

Serves 4.

The Missouri Peach Fair

Since the American Legion C. Dolph Gehrig Post sponsored the first Peach Festival in 1944, Campbell has held an annual event celebrating the harvest of the local peaches, for which this area is justifiably well-known. In the 1960's, the event was recognized as an official Missouri function and is now called the Missouri Peach Fair.

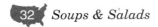

Lobster Tail & Watermelon Salad

Missouri-Arkansas Watermelon Association—Kennett

4 LOBSTER TAILS, cooked
2 cups 1/2-inch WATERMELON cubes
2 AVOCADOS, peeled and cut into 1/2-inch cubes
2 PAPAYAS, cut into 1/2-inch cubes
1/2 cup chopped fresh CILANTRO
1/2 cup fresh LEMON JUICE
1 1/2 cups SALAD OIL
2 Tbsp. HONEY
1 Tbsp. JERK SEASONING
SALT and PEPPER
1 head ICEBERG LETTUCE, shredded
1 oz. COCONUT FLAKES

Cut lobster tails in half lengthwise; devein. Cut into 1/2-inch slices. In a bowl, combine lobster, watermelon, avocados, papayas and cilantro. Pour lemon juice into a small bowl and slowly whisk in oil; stir in honey, jerk seasoning and salt and pepper to taste. Pour dressing over lobster mixture and refrigerate for 1 hour, stirring occasionally. Place lobster mixture on a bed of lettuce and sprinkle with coconut.

Serves 6.

Classic Waldorf Salad

Missouri Apple Merchandising Council—Columbia

3 cups diced TART APPLES
1/2 cup chopped CELERY
3/4 cup halved WHITE GRAPES
1/2 cup chopped PECANS

1/4 cup RAISINS
3/4 cup MAYONNAISE
1 Tbsp. SUGAR
1/2 tsp. LEMON JUICE

Combine apples, celery, grapes, pecans and raisins in a large serving bowl. Combine mayonnaise, sugar and lemon juice. Fold dressing into fruit. Chill.

Serves 6.

Wonderful
Black Walnut Salad

Dwain Hammons—Hammons Products Company, Stockton

2 cups MISSOURI DANDY® BLACK WALNUTS
2 Tbsp. BUTTER
1 Tbsp. SEASONED SALT
2 heads BOSTON or BUTTER LETTUCE, torn into large pieces
1/2 cup chopped PARSLEY
2 cans (14 oz. ea.) HEARTS OF PALM, drained and sliced
1/4-1/2 lb. BLUE CHEESE, crumbled

Preheat oven to 350°. Place walnuts on a baking sheet and dot with butter; sprinkle with seasoned salt. Toast in the oven for 10 minutes. Arrange lettuce on salad plates; sprinkle with parsley. Evenly place hearts of palm, blue cheese and walnuts over the lettuce. Drizzle ***Black Walnut Vinaigrette Dressing*** over each salad.

Serves 8.

Black Walnut Vinaigrette Dressing

1 3/4 cups VEGETABLE OIL
1/4 cup BLACK WALNUT OIL
1 cup VINEGAR
1/4 cup SUGAR
1/2 tsp. GARLIC POWDER
SALT and PEPPER

In a bowl, combine all ingredients, seasoning with salt and pepper to taste. Pour mixture into a jar. Seal and shake to mix. May be refrigerated for up to two weeks.

Independence

This northwestern Missouri city was the hometown of President Harry S. Truman and is one of the state's most historic cities. The Oregon and Santa Fe trails began here, establishing it as the "Gateway to the West" for pioneers in the mid-1800s.

Western Beef & Pasta Salad

Wheat Foods Council—Columbia

8 oz. WAGON WHEELS, ROTINI or other medium-sized PASTA
2 Tbsp. VEGETABLE OIL
3 Tbsp. LEMON JUICE
2 Tbsp. RED WINE VINEGAR
2 Tbsp. DIJON MUSTARD
1 tsp. OREGANO
1 tsp. THYME
1/4 cup chopped fresh PARSLEY
4 oz. fresh MUSHROOMS, sliced
6 oz. cooked LEAN ROAST BEEF, julienne
1 cup SNOW PEAS, chopped into 1/2-inch pieces
1/2 RED BELL PEPPER, chopped
1/2 YELLOW BELL PEPPER, chopped
SALT
Freshly ground PEPPER

Prepare pasta according to package directions; drain. Rinse in cold water and drain thoroughly. In a large glass or ceramic bowl, mix oil, lemon juice, vinegar, mustard, oregano, thyme, parsley, mushrooms and beef. Toss with snow peas, bell peppers and pasta; mix thoroughly. Season with salt and pepper to taste. Refrigerate for 1 hour and serve.

Serves 6.

Columbia

Made the seat of Boone County in 1821, this town became a prosperous outfitting station for westbound emigrants when Boone's Lick Trail was rerouted through the area. The University of Missouri, the first public university west of the Mississippi River, opened its doors here in 1839. The University's Ellis Library houses the State Historical Society of Missouri.

Sirloin Salad with Dried Cranberries

Missouri Beef Industry Council—Columbia

1 lb. BEEF TOP SIRLOIN STEAK, cut 1-inch thick
1 tsp. KOSHER SALT
2 tsp. coarsely ground PEPPER
2 heads BOSTON LETTUCE, torn into bite-size pieces
1/2 cup BLUE CHEESE, crumbled
1/2 cup dried CRANBERRIES
1/2 cup PINE NUTS, toasted

Dressing:
  2 Tbsp. ORANGE JUICE
  2 Tbsp. RED WINE VINEGAR
  1 Tbsp. OLIVE OIL
  2 tsp. HONEY
  1 1/4 tsp. DIJON MUSTARD

Rub steak with salt and pepper. Grill over medium-hot coals for 14 minutes for medium-rare doneness. Place lettuce in a large salad bowl or on a platter. Sprinkle with Blue cheese, cranberries and pine nuts. To prepare dressing: In a bowl, whisk together dressing ingredients until slightly thickened. Carve steak at an angle across the grain into 1/4-inch thick slices, cut 2-inches long and place over lettuce. Drizzle with dressing and serve at once.

Serves 4.

Winemaking in Missouri

Founded in 1832, Dutzow became one of Missouri's first wine-making towns and in the 1890's, Stone Hill Winery in Hermann became the nation's third largest winery. Before 1920, Stone Hill was the second largest wine producer in the U.S. Prohibition in the 1920's however caused many wineries to pull up their grapes and close. Stone Hill grew mushrooms in its huge cellars until 1967. Today there are more than twenty-five wineries in Missouri, making many varieties of sweet and dry wines and even champagne!

Garden Slaw

1 GREEN BELL PEPPER, slivered	2 cups grated CARROTS
8 cups shredded CABBAGE	1/2 cup chopped ONION
	1/2 cup WATER, divided

In a bowl, combine bell pepper, cabbage, carrots and onion. Sprinkle with 1/2 cup water and chill. When ready to serve, drain vegetables and toss with *Celery Seed Dressing.*

Celery Seed Dressing

1 pkg. (1 oz.) UNFLAVORED GELATIN	2 tsp. CELERY SEED
1/4 cup water	1 1/2 tsp. SALT
2/3 cup SUGAR	1/4 tsp. PEPPER
2/3 cup VINEGAR	2/3 cup SALAD OIL

In a bowl, dissolve gelatin in 1/4 cup water; set aside. In a saucepan, combine sugar, vinegar, celery seed, salt and pepper and bring to a boil. Stir in gelatin. Cool mixture until slightly thickened then beat well. Beat in salad oil gradually.

Serves 6-8.

New Madrid

The most powerful earthquake to strike the nation occurred in 1811 and was centered in this southeast city. The quake shook more than one million square miles and vibrations were felt from the Rocky Mountains to the Atlantic Coast and from Canada to Mexico.

Turnip Salad

3 cups shredded TURNIPS	1 cup shredded CARROTS
1/2 cup RAISINS	1 cup MAYONNAISE
1 Tbsp. LEMON JUICE	

In a large bowl, combine all ingredients and mix well. Chill for at least one hour before serving.

Hot German Potato Salad

Julia K. McMillan—Kansas City

1-1 1/2 lbs. POTATOES
1 tsp. SALT
1/8 tsp. PEPPER
1/2 tsp. SUGAR
1/2 tsp. FLOUR
1/2 cup WATER

1/2 cup VINEGAR
1/4 lb. sliced BACON,
    finely chopped
1 med. ONION, finely
    chopped
1 tsp. MUSTARD

Place potatoes in a large saucepan and add enough water to cover. Boil potatoes until tender; drain. While hot, peel and cut potatoes into 1/4-inch slices. Sprinkle salt, pepper, sugar and flour over potatoes; set aside. In a saucepan, combine water and vinegar and heat thoroughly. In a large skillet, cook bacon until brown. Add onion and let brown slightly, then add potato mixture. Pour vinegar mixture over all and let heat through to absorb liquid. Stir in mustard. Transfer to serving dish.

Did You Know?
Iced tea was invented by Richard Blechyden at the St. Louis World's Fair in 1904!

Frozen Strawberry Salad

*"I make this salad every Thanksgiving.
It is a family favorite!"*

Mrs. B.J. (Glenna) Garber—Carthage

1 ctn. (8 oz.) FAT FREE COOL WHIP®
1 can (14 oz.) SWEETENED CONDENSED MILK
1 pkg. (12 oz.) FROZEN STRAWBERRIES,
    thawed
1 can (20 oz.) CRUSHED PINEAPPLE
3 BANANAS, diced
LETTUCE LEAVES

In a bowl, mix cool whip and milk together. Add strawberries and pineapple with their juice. Fold in bananas. Place mixture in a 13 x 9 glass dish; cover and freeze. Let stand 5-10 minutes before serving. Cut into small squares and serve over a lettuce leaf.

Main Dishes

Beef Brisket Kansas City-Style

"Kansas City is known for its beef. Some of the best beef in the country still comes through the stockyards of this heartland city! Our beef brisket is marinated in KC Masterpiece® Barbecue Sauce, a locally 'brewed' favorite, and then it is slow roasted."

Cynthia Brogdon—The Doanleigh Inn, Kansas City

1 (3-4 lb.) BEEF BRISKET
3 Tbsp. minced GARLIC
1 Tbsp. VEGETABLE OIL
3 cups KC MASTERPIECE® BARBECUE SAUCE

Trim brisket, then spread garlic over meat. In a large, heavy skillet, heat oil and brown brisket on both sides. Transfer brisket to a large roasting pan and cover with barbecue sauce. Tightly cover the pan with foil. Bake at 350° for 2-3 hours or until very tender. Slice and serve with additional barbecue sauce.

Marvelous Meatloaf

"I developed this recipe in an effort to use only fresh, local ingredients for family meals. We raise beef, a neighbor raises pork, another has eggs and onions and our bread comes from a nearby commune. I usually cook without salt or pepper because fresh ingredients have so much flavor!"

Margot McMillen—Timber Hill Farm, Fulton

2 lbs. GROUND BEEF
1 lb. GROUND PORK
1/4 cup chopped RED ONION
2 EGGS, lightly beaten
3 cups BREAD CRUMBS
3 cups diced fresh or home-canned TOMATOES

In a large bowl, combine all ingredients and mix thoroughly. Divide mixture and shape into two loaves; place loaves on a broiler pan. Bake at 350° for one hour or until the center is no longer pink.

Kirksville

This northern Missouri town was founded in 1841 by Jesse Kirk, who exchanged a turkey dinner for the right to name the town after himself.

Holiday Wild Turkey

1 cup chopped ONIONS
1 cup chopped CELERY
1/8 cup OIL
1 cube CHICKEN BOUILLON
1/2 cup HOT WATER
1 EGG

1 pkg. (12 oz.) SEASONED STUFFING MIX
1 WILD TURKEY
6 slices BACON
2 cups WATER

In a skillet, sauté onions and celery in oil until crisp tender. Dissolve bouillon cube in water, add to skillet. Add stuffing mix and egg and stir well. Rinse and dry turkey inside and out; stuff with dressing. Place on rack in roasting pan and arrange bacon over breast and legs. Add 2 cups water to pan. Bake at 300° for 4 hours, basting every 30 minutes with drippings. Uncover and bake 30 minutes more.

My Spaghetti Red

"There is a very unique diner in Joplin, Fred & Red's, that is famous for its Spaghetti Red. I made up this recipe in hopes of capturing the taste for our enjoyment."

Pam Whyte—Prosperity School Bed & Breakfast, Joplin

2 lbs. GROUND CHUCK	2 cans (8 oz. ea.) WATER
1 pkg. (1.25 oz.) CHILI SEASONING	1 pkg. (16 oz.) SPAGHETTI
1 tsp. SALT	Chopped DILL PICKLES
1 tsp. CUMIN	Sliced ONION, optional
3 cans (8 oz. ea.) TOMATO SAUCE	KETCHUP, optional

In a large skillet, brown beef; drain. Stir in seasonings, tomato sauce and water and simmer over medium heat for 30 minutes. Cook spaghetti according to package directions; drain. Spoon sauce over bed of pasta. Top with pickles, onion and ketchup.

Chicken Vermicelli

"This recipe is delicious and yet so easy to prepare."

Thomas A. Tucker—Vivienne® Dressings/Tucker Food Products, Inc., St. Louis

4 boneless, skinless CHICKEN BREASTS
WATER
1 Tbsp. SALT
1 pkg. (16 oz.) VERMICELLI PASTA
1/2 cup julienne GREEN BELL PEPPER
4 oz. VIVIENNE® ROMANO CHEESE DRESSING

Place chicken breasts in a 6-quart kettle and add enough water to cover. Bring to a boil and cook for 5-7 minutes. Remove chicken from kettle and set aside. Add salt to boiling water and cook pasta al dente; drain well. Julienne the chicken while pasta is cooking. Combine chicken, bell pepper and pasta in a large bowl; stir in dressing and toss.

Serves 4-6.

Grandma's Favorite Pork Roast

"This recipe's secret ingredient is A Taste of the Kingdom® Pepper Jelly made by our family of Callawegians who live in a real kingdom where we make our products from produce grown on our family farm."

Julie Jones Price—A Taste of the Kingdom, LLC, Kingdom City

1 (3-5 lb.) PORK ROAST
A TASTE OF THE KINGDOM® PEPPER JELLY

Score roast with 1/4-inch deep cuts in criss-cross style and place in a baking pan. Bake at 325° for 35 minutes per pound. One-half hour before roast is done, brush generously with pepper jelly, making sure cuts are filled with jelly. Return to oven and continue baking. A delicious glaze will form from the jelly as it bakes.

Note: Heat pepper jelly in microwave for smoother spreading.

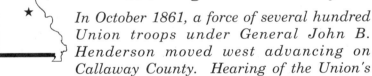

The Kingdom of Callaway

In October 1861, a force of several hundred Union troops under General John B. Henderson moved west advancing on Callaway County. Hearing of the Union's advance, Colonel Jefferson F. Jones quickly mustered his own army composed of determined old men and boys. The Callawegians marched east to meet the Union force, dragging along with them wooden logs shaped and painted to resemble artillery pieces. They deployed these "cannons" along the county line and built extra camp fires to make the Union General believe his opposition was stronger than it really was. The ruse worked and not a shot was fired! A treaty was signed and ever since, Callawegians have been proud to call their home "The Kingdom of Callaway."

Simply Delicious Pork Chops

"My mother used to make this recipe a lot. My father raised hogs so we had pork all the time."

Nancy Rezabek—Columbia

6 PORK CHOPS

Marinade:

2 Tbsp. OIL

2 Tbsp. KETCHUP

1 Tbsp. LEMON JUICE

1 Tbsp. WORCESTERSHIRE SAUCE

1 Tbsp. SOY SAUCE

Arrange pork chops in a 13 x 9 glass baking dish. In a small bowl, combine marinade ingredients and pour over pork chops, turning once to coat well. Cover and marinate in refrigerator for several hours or overnight. Bake, covered, at 325° for 1 hour; uncover and bake for an additional 30 minutes or until tender.

So-Easy Chili

"This is an easy-to-make family favorite."

Georgia L. Snider—Chaffee

3 lbs. GROUND BEEF

1 ONION, chopped

2 (16 oz. ea.) RICE'S® CHILI ROLLS

4 cans (10.75 oz. ea.) TOMATO SOUP

3 cans (15.5 oz. ea.) KIDNEY BEANS, drained

5 cans (15 oz. ea.) CHILI BEANS, drained

1 can (14.5 oz.) STEWED TOMATOES

1 qt. WATER

2 Tbsp. CHILI POWDER

3/4 Tbsp. GARLIC POWDER

1 can (10 oz.) diced ROTEL® TOMATO AND GREEN CHILES

2 tsp. ONION POWDER

ONION SALT

In an 8-quart soup kettle, brown beef with onion; drain well. Stir in remaining ingredients and simmer for 30 minutes. Season with onion salt to taste.

Serves 14-16.

Johnny Come Lately

"This recipe is from my mother who got it from her mother. We don't know where the name came from, but it has been a favorite family dinner for years!"

Karen Forney—Victorian Veranda Bed & Breakfast, Bonne Terre

1 pkg. (7 oz.) EGG NOODLES	1 jar (7 oz.) STUFFED
1 can (4 oz.) TOMATO SAUCE	OLIVES, diced
1 1/2 lbs. GROUND BEEF	1 can (10.75 oz.) TOMATO
1 ONION, minced	SOUP
1/4 tsp. SALT	1 lb. VELVEETA®, sliced
1/4 tsp. PEPPER	

Cook noodles according to package directions. Drain and place in a buttered 13 x 9 casserole dish. Spread tomato sauce on top of noodles. In a large skillet, brown beef with onion; drain. Season with salt and pepper. Pour beef mixture on top of tomato sauce and sprinkle with olives. Spread tomato soup over olives and arrange cheese on top. Cover with foil and bake at 350° for 1 hour.

Serves 8.

Steak Rauseo

Nancy Rauseo—Mariah Acres, Cameron

1 (3 lb.) SIRLOIN or T-BONE STEAK	1 tsp. minced GARLIC
1/2 cup FLOUR	Dash of HOT SAUCE
2 Tbsp. BUTTER	JUICE of 1/2 LEMON
1 can (2 oz.) ANCHOVIES	Fresh PARSLEY
1 Tbsp. CAPERS	PEPPER

Cut meat from bone, filet steak in half from 1/4 to 3/8-inch thickness to create 4-6 medallions. Dredge steak in flour. In a large skillet, melt butter over medium heat and brown steak on one side; turn and raise heat. Add anchovies, capers, garlic and hot sauce; cook until anchovies dissolve. When serving, drizzle with lemon juice; sprinkle with parsley and pepper.

Serves 4.

Pork Tenderloin Medallions with Cinnamon Couscous & Peach Chutney

Missouri Pork Producers Association—Columbia

1 (1 lb.) PORK TENDERLOIN	1 Tbsp. CUMIN
1 tsp. SALT	1 Tbsp. CHILI POWDER
2 tsp. PEPPER	

Cut pork tenderloin into medallions about 3/4-inch thick. In a bowl, combine salt, pepper, cumin and chili powder; rub mixture into medallions. Medallions may be cooked immediately or covered and refrigerated overnight. Grill or broil medallions 4-5 minutes per side. Serve medallions with *Cinnamon Couscous* and *Peach Chutney*.

Cinnamon Couscous

2 1/2 cups WATER	2 Tbsp. BUTTER
1 tsp. CINNAMON	1 1/2 cups COUSCOUS
1 tsp. SALT	

In a large saucepan, bring water, cinnamon, salt and butter to a boil; stir in couscous. Cover and let rest until all water has been absorbed (about 10 minutes).

Peach Chutney

1/2 RED BELL PEPPER, diced
1 clove GARLIC, minced
1/2 RED ONION, diced
1 JALAPEÑO PEPPER, seeded and diced
1 can (16 oz.) PEACH SLICES, drained
2 Tbsp. BROWN SUGAR
2 Tbsp. RED WINE VINEGAR

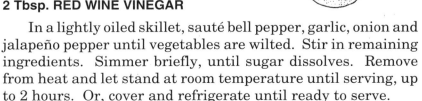

In a lightly oiled skillet, sauté bell pepper, garlic, onion and jalapeño pepper until vegetables are wilted. Stir in remaining ingredients. Simmer briefly, until sugar dissolves. Remove from heat and let stand at room temperature until serving, up to 2 hours. Or, cover and refrigerate until ready to serve.

Missouri
Sugar Cured Ham

"This was the way my late dad, John C. Davis, cured the hams to feed 12 children—with mother's help, of course!"

Lillie Kraemer—Jackson

3/4 cup packed BROWN SUGAR
1 Tbsp. CAYENNE
3 Tbsp. PEPPER

2 cups CANNING SALT
1 (25 lb.) HAM

In a small mixing bowl, combine brown sugar, cayenne, pepper and salt. Saw the shank from the ham. Place a regular size feed sack on a table; cover sack with 4 staggered layers of newspaper. Sprinkle 1/4 cup of the seasoning mixture on the paper and lay the skin side of the ham on top. Rub remaining mixture over the ham until all the meat is covered. Carefully fold the papers tightly around the ham. Roll the sack down to the ham and keep pulling and twisting to get the cloth very tight. Tie the two ends of the cloth and let the ham lay for 3 days, skin side down, before hanging it to cure. The ham is ready to eat in 3-6 months.

Ronnie's Hot Ribs

Ronnie Alewel—Missouri Association of Meat Processors, Sedalia

3 lbs. RIBS

Basting Sauce:
2 ONIONS, finely chopped
2 Tbsp. VINEGAR
2 Tbsp. WORCESTERSHIRE
   SAUCE
1 Tbsp. SALT
1/2 tsp. PAPRIKA

1/8 tsp. CAYENNE
1/4 tsp. PEPPER
1/2 tsp. CHILI POWDER
3/4 cup KETCHUP
3/4 cup WATER
2 Tbsp. BROWN SUGAR

Arrange ribs in a single layer in a foil-lined pan. Combine basting sauce ingredients in a medium bowl; mix well. Pour over ribs. Bake, uncovered, at 350° for 2 1/2 hours; baste often.

Mom's Meatloaf

"The many spices used in the traditional Bloody Mary cocktail greatly enhance the flavors of many recipes. When I was a boy, my father taught me how to make the cocktail to serve to our guests. I later decided to create and bottle my own version of the mix...Redbird Gourmet Bloody Mary Mix. I added jalapeño peppers for an extra 'kick.'"

Stan Squires—Halben Foods, St. Louis

2 EGGS
1/4 cup MILK
2 lbs. GROUND CHUCK
1/2 lb. GROUND PORK or ITALIAN SAUSAGE
1/4 cup CRACKER CRUMBS or OATMEAL
1/2 tsp. minced GARLIC
1/2 sm. GREEN BELL PEPPER, finely chopped
1 med. ONION, finely chopped
1/2 tsp. ITALIAN SEASONING
1/2 tsp. CELERY SALT
1 tsp. PARSLEY FLAKES
12 oz. REDBIRD® GOURMET BLOODY MARY MIX, divided

In a bowl, stir together eggs and milk. In a large mixing bowl, combine remaining ingredients, except for Bloody Mary mix. Gradually add egg mixture to meat mixture, kneading thoroughly between additions. Blend in 1/2 of the Bloody Mary mix. Place meat mixture in a loaf pan and bake at 325° for 30 minutes. Remove from oven and top with remaining Bloody Mary mix. Return to oven and bake for another 30 minutes.

St. Louis

St. Louis was named after King Louis IX. During the first half of the 1800s, St. Louis served as a gateway to the West and as a main port for Mississippi River steamboats. The Jefferson National Expansion Memorial stands on the riverfront and includes the famous 630-foot Gateway Arch, the nation's tallest monument.

Maull's Sweet-n-Smoky Barbecue Brisket

Michael Hixson—Louis Maull Co., St. Louis

SALT and PEPPER
1 (4 lb.) BEEF BRISKET
3 cups MAULL'S® SWEET-N-SMOKY BARBECUE SAUCE, divided

Salt and pepper brisket to taste and place in a large casserole dish. Pour 2 cups of barbecue sauce over meat; cover and refrigerate overnight. Cook, covered, at 250° for 4 hours. Thinly slice meat and return slices to the pan; add remaining barbecue sauce. Bake, uncovered, at 300° for 30 minutes.

Daddy Buck's Lil' Grillers

Nancy Scott—Daddy Buck's Inc., Linn Creek

1/2 cup GARLIC POWDER
1/4 cup PEPPER
1/4 cup SEASONED SALT
1/4 cup CELERY SALT
1 (5 lb.) BEEF BRISKET, thinly sliced
1 cup finely chopped ONION
20 slices AMERICAN CHEESE
1 lb. sliced BACON
DADDY BUCK'S® HICKORY
    SMOKED BBQ & DIPPING SAUCE

In a bowl, combine garlic powder, pepper, seasoned salt and celery salt; mix well. Lay a slice of brisket on a wood cutting board. Generously sprinkle spice mix and onion on meat. Pound meat thin with a meat tenderizer. Cut slices of cheese no wider than meat. Lay cheese on meat and roll up jelly roll style. Wrap a slice of bacon on outside of meat roll and secure with a toothpick. Repeat process with remaining brisket. Grill rolls at medium heat for 30 minutes; baste with barbecue sauce and grill for 5 minutes longer. Turn, baste again and grill for an additional 5 minutes.

Makes approximately 25 grillers.

Mexicana Casserole

Missouri Soybean Merchandising Council—Jefferson City

1 lb. GROUND CHUCK
3/4 cup chopped ONION
1 cup cooked SOYBEANS
4 lg. EGGS
1 can (5 oz.) EVAPORATED MILK
1/2 cup SILKEN EXTRA-FIRM TOFU
1 pkg. (1.25 oz.) TACO SEASONING MIX
1 can (8 oz.) TOMATO SAUCE
2 cups crushed CORN CHIPS
1 1/2 cups shredded CHEDDAR CHEESE
2 cups chopped ICEBERG LETTUCE
1 med. TOMATO, chopped
1/4 cup BLACK OLIVES, sliced
1 cup SALSA
1/2 cup SOUR CREAM

Preheat oven to 350°. In a skillet, brown ground chuck and onions. Place in bottom of a 13 x 9 baking dish. Top with soybeans. In a bowl, beat together eggs, milk, tofu, taco seasoning and tomato sauce; pour over soybeans. Sprinkle corn chips over top and bake for 25 minutes. Add cheese to top and bake for 5 more minutes. Cool 5-10 minutes. In a bowl, stir together lettuce, tomato, olives and salsa; sprinkle over casserole. Top with dollops of sour cream and serve.

Mexican Foods

Mexicans have lived and worked in Missouri since the days of the Santa Fe Trail. Mexican cooking, with its bold and earthy flavors, is a blend of many cultures— Native American, Spanish, Portuguese, French and African. The most important ingredients in Mexican cooking are beans, chile peppers, tomatoes, beef, pork, rice and cheese. Corn, used in making tortillas, tamales and breads is a mainstay. Herbs and spices such as coriander, oregano and cinnamon provide spicy accents to their simple foods.

Nellie's Southern Fried Chicken

"My mother was originally from Norway but settled in the Carthage area in the late 1800s. Everyone in our family loves this chicken dish."

Mary Jo Hancock—Scott City

1/2 cup FLOUR
1/4 tsp. PEPPER
1/2 tsp. ROSEMARY
1/2 tsp. CHILI POWDER
1/2 tsp. THYME
1/2 tsp. CURRY POWDER
1/2 tsp. PAPRIKA

1/2 tsp. GINGER
1/2 tsp. POULTRY SPICE
  SEASONING
1 FRYING CHICKEN,
  cut into pieces
OIL for frying

In a plastic bag, combine all ingredients except for chicken and oil and mix well. Place chicken in bag, one piece at a time, and shake until well-coated. In a deep skillet, heat 1-inch of oil to 370°. Place chicken in skillet in a single layer and cook until submerged side is brown and tender, about 12 minutes. Turn and cook until brown and tender on the other side, about 12 minutes. Chicken is done when its juices run clear.

Oven Stew

"My sister gave me this recipe—it really comes in handy when you have to be gone all afternoon!"

Nancy Rezabek—Columbia

2 lbs. STEW MEAT (do not brown)
5 med. CARROTS, cut into 2-inch pieces
4 POTATOES, cut into 2-inch pieces
8 oz. fresh MUSHROOMS
1 lg. ONION, diced
2 1/2 cups V-8® JUICE
1/4 cup MINUTE TAPIOCA
1/2 tsp. SEASONED SALT
1/4 tsp. PEPPER
1/2 tsp. BASIL

Combine all ingredients in a 6-quart casserole dish and mix gently. Cover and bake at 275° for 5 hours.

Broccoli Casserole

Missouri Soybean Merchandising Council—Jefferson City

1/2 cup chopped ONION
1 Tbsp. SOY MARGARINE
1 bag (16 oz.) frozen CHOPPED BROCCOLI
1/2 lb. AMERICAN CHEESE, cubed
3 cups cooked RICE
1 cup firm TOFU, cubed
1 can (10.75 oz.) CREAM of MUSHROOM SOUP
1 can (10.75 oz.) CREAM of CHICKEN SOUP
1/4 cup BREAD CRUMBS

Preheat oven to 375°. In a skillet, sauté onion in soy margarine. In a saucepan, cook broccoli until tender; stir in cheese until completely melted. In a large bowl, combine onions, rice, broccoli/cheese mixture, tofu and soups; mix well. Spray a 10 x 10 baking dish with cooking spray; spread broccoli mixture evenly in dish. Sprinkle bread crumbs over top and bake for 20 minutes.

Standing Rib Roast

"This recipe really creates a delicious roast. Start roast (any size) in the morning and reheat as directed in the last step of the recipe, just in time for dinner."

Ronnie Alewel—Missouri Association of Meat Processors, Sedalia

1 STANDING BEEF RIB ROAST
SALT and PEPPER

Let roast stand at room temperature for at least 1 hour (if roast is frozen, thaw completely.) Preheat oven to 375°. Rub roast with salt and pepper to taste. Place roast rib-side down on roasting pan rack and bake for 1 hour; turn off oven. Allow roast to remain in the oven and *do not open the door!* Thirty to forty minutes before serving, bring oven to 375° and cook roast for 30-40 minutes for rare meat; add 15-30 minutes for a more well-done roast.

Chicken & Baked Dumplings

"I did not like the chicken pot pie recipes I tried, so I came up with this one. It is also a great way to use up leftover turkey after Thanksgiving. Our family really enjoys this one-dish meal."

Mrs. B.J. (Glenna) Garber—Carthage

1/2 cup BUTTER or MARGARINE
1/2 cup FLOUR
1 tsp. SALT
1/2 tsp. PEPPER
4 cups CHICKEN BROTH
1 can (12 oz.) EVAPORATED MILK
2 cans (16 oz. ea.) MIXED VEGETABLES, drained
4 cups diced cooked CHICKEN or TURKEY

Melt butter in a large saucepan. Stir in flour and seasonings; mix well. Add chicken broth and evaporated milk; cook slowly until mixture thickens. Gently stir in vegetables and chicken and heat thoroughly. Place chicken mixture in a serving dish and arrange ***Baked Dumplings*** on top.

Baked Dumplings

2 cups FLOUR   **3/4 cup SHORTENING**
1 tsp. SALT   **5 Tbsp. COLD WATER**

Combine flour and salt in a mixing bowl; cut in shortening until mixture is crumbly. Sprinkle with water one tablespoon at a time. Toss lightly with a fork until dough forms into a ball. Roll out onto a floured surface. Cut with a biscuit cutter or desired cookie cutter shape. Place on a cookie sheet and prick with a fork. Bake at 350° for 10 minutes.

Jesse James

Jesse James, the infamous bank and train robber was born in 1847 in Clay County. Jesse and his gang, which included his brother Frank, always carried the stolen money off in grain sacks. After moving to St. Joseph, Jesse James was shot and killed by a newcomer to his gang who sought the $10,000 reward placed on his head.

Fresh Garden Spaghetti

"Fifty years ago Dallas County was a major producer and processor of tomatoes. Now that legacy is carried on by only a handful of family farms like ours. This recipe was created to take advantage of the wonderful tomatoes and other produce grown in our gardens."

Cheryl Compton—Compton Family Farm, Tunas

2 Tbsp. OLIVE OIL
3/4 cup finely chopped EGGPLANT
2 CARROTS, finely chopped
1 med. ONION, finely chopped
1 GREEN BELL PEPPER, finely chopped
1-2 cloves GARLIC, minced
3 Tbsp. chopped fresh BASIL or
    1 Tbsp. crushed DRIED BASIL
3 Tbsp. chopped fresh OREGANO or
    1 Tbsp. crushed dried OREGANO
1 1/2 cups chopped TOMATOES
1 can (15 oz.) TOMATO SAUCE
SALT
SPAGHETTI SQUASH or PASTA

In a large skillet, heat oil and sauté eggplant, carrots, onion, bell pepper and garlic until slightly soft; add basil and oregano and sauté for 3-5 minutes. Stir in tomatoes, tomato sauce and salt to taste; bring to a boil. Serve over ***Baked Spaghetti Squash*** or pasta.

Baked Spaghetti Squash

Split squash in half, remove pulp and place open side down in a shallow pan filled with 1-inch of water. Bake squash at 400° for 30 minutes.

Boonville
The first battle of the Civil War in Missouri was fought here on June 17, 1861 when Union troops under General Lyon defeated state troops led by Governor Jackson.

Gourmet Tomato Stew

Stan Squires—Halben Foods, St. Louis

1 cup cooked and shredded ROAST BEEF
3 cups REDBIRD® GOURMET BLOODY MARY MIX
2 cups WATER
1 1/2 cups diced CELERY
1 1/2 cups peeled and diced POTATOES
3/4 cup sliced STUFFED SPANISH
    GREEN OLIVES
2 Tbsp. diced YELLOW ONION
2 Tbsp. WORCESTERSHIRE SAUCE
1/4 tsp. PEPPER
2 Tbsp. SUGAR
1 LEMON, sliced

In a large soup kettle, combine all ingredients except lemon slices. Bring to a boil; reduce heat and simmer for 30 minutes. Garnish with lemon slices floating on top when serving.

Serves 6-8.

Did You Know?

Begun in 1922, Country Club Plaza in Kansas City was America's first suburban shopping district.

Veggie Stroganoff

"This is a family favorite and very easy to fix."

Cheryl Compton—Compton Family Farm, Tunas

1 Tbsp. OLIVE OIL
1 ONION, finely chopped
2 CARROTS, finely chopped
3 stalks CELERY, finely chopped
1 cup sliced MUSHROOMS
1 lg. clove GARLIC, minced

1/8 tsp. PEPPER
2 cups puréed TOMATOES
1 can (10.75 oz.) CREAM OF
    MUSHROOM SOUP
1/2 cup SOUR CREAM
RICE or PASTA

In a skillet, heat oil. Add onion, carrots, celery and mushrooms; stir. Add garlic and pepper and sauté mixture until vegetables are tender. Stir in tomatoes, soup and sour cream and cook until heated thoroughly. Serve over rice or pasta.

Side Dishes

Squash Casserole

"We grow lots of squash here in Missouri! This is a great casserole dish to take to family gatherings."

Martha M. Darrough—Farmington

6 cups sliced **YELLOW or ZUCCHINI SQUASH**
1/4 cup chopped **ONION**
1 can (10.75 oz.) **CREAM OF CHICKEN SOUP**
1 cup **SOUR CREAM**
1 cup shredded **CARROTS**
1/2 cup **BUTTER**
1 pkg. (6 oz.) **HERB STUFFING MIX**

In a saucepan, bring 6 cups of water to a boil. Add squash and onion; boil for 5 minutes, then drain. In a mixing bowl, combine soup, sour cream and carrots; fold into squash and onion mixture. Melt butter and combine with stuffing mix. Place 1/2 of the stuffing mixture in the bottom of a 12 x 8 baking dish. Pour squash mixture over stuffing mixture and top with remaining stuffing mixture. Bake at 350° for 30 minutes.

My Favorite Zucchini Casserole

"In our produce business, customers often share favorite recipes. Of all the zucchini recipes I've received, this is my favorite. It is easy to make because I have modified it to cook completely on top of the stove. The taste is unbeatable!"

Jo Ann Blackwell—Blackwell Family Produce, Salem

4 slices BACON	**2 cups chopped ZUCCHINI**
1/4 cup chopped ONION	**2 cups chopped TOMATOES**
1/4 cup chopped CELERY	**1/8 tsp. OREGANO**
1/4 cup chopped GREEN	**1/4 tsp. PEPPER**
BELL PEPPER	**1 1/2 tsp. SALT**
1/2 cup uncooked INSTANT	**1/8 tsp. THYME**
RICE	**1 cup shredded CHEESE**

In a large skillet, fry bacon until crisp; remove and reserve drippings. Sauté onion, celery and bell pepper in bacon drippings until tender. Add rice and stir well to coat. Stir in zucchini, tomatoes and seasonings. Cover and cook until rice is tender. Sprinkle with cheese and cover until cheese melts. Crumble bacon over casserole before serving.

Note: Yellow squash may also be used for this casserole.

Zucchini Tips

Using Zucchini & Summer Squash

Try some of the following ideas for using zucchini:
• Serve sliced, with other vegetables, for an appetizer or snack • Slice into tossed vegetable salads • Add to any stir-fry dish • Shred into bread or muffin mix • Shred and add to meatloaves for added nutritional value.

Preserving Zucchini & Summer Squash

To Freeze: Select 5 to 7-inch long squash. Wash and cut into pieces. Blanch. Chill immediately in ice water, pack in freezer containers.

Green Rice

"A good friend gave this recipe to me 20 years ago. I grow parsley in my garden during the summer, then I chop and freeze it for use in the winter in recipes like this."

Dortha J. Strack—Cape Girardeau

1 Tbsp. + 1/4 cup VEGETABLE OIL, divided
1 sm. ONION, chopped
1/2 cup chopped CELERY
1 cup chopped PARSLEY
1 cup cooked RICE
2 EGGS, beaten
2 cups MILK
1 lb. VELVEETA®, cubed
SALT and PEPPER

PARSLEY

In a skillet, heat 1 tablespoon oil and sauté onion, celery and parsley until onion is translucent. In a bowl, combine rice, eggs, 1/4 cup oil, milk and cheese; season with salt and pepper to taste. Stir in onion mixture and pour into a greased baking dish. Bake at 350° for 1 hour.

Baked Shoestring Potatoes

"This is a 'must serve' at family gatherings!"

Ronnie Alewel—Sedalia

4 med. POTATOES
3 Tbsp. BUTTER
1 1/2 tsp. SALT
Dash of PEPPER
2 Tbsp. chopped PARSLEY

1/2 cup grated CHEDDAR
    CHEESE
1/2 cup HEAVY CREAM (no
    substitution)

Cut potatoes in thin, lengthwise strips and place in a baking dish. Dot with butter and sprinkle with salt, pepper, parsley and cheese. Pour cream over mixture. Bake, covered, at 450° for 1 hour.

Spinach-Zucchini Casserole

"My mother-in-law, Ceal Wilder of Ste. Genevieve, gave me this recipe many years ago. She said it was her favorite vegetable casserole recipe. It is a hit every time I fix it for our family."

Verona L. Wilder—Marble Hill

3 Tbsp. VEGETABLE OIL
1 ONION, chopped
1/2 clove GARLIC, minced
1 tsp. OREGANO
1 tsp. PARSLEY
1/2 tsp. SALT
1 med. ZUCCHINI, peeled and chunked
1 cup cooked SPINACH
3 EGGS, beaten
2/3 cup BREAD CRUMBS
1/2-3/4 cup PARMESAN CHEESE

In a skillet, heat oil and sauté onion, garlic, oregano, parsley and salt until onion is translucent. Place zucchini in a blender and purée. In a bowl, combine onion mixture with spinach, zucchini and eggs; mix well. Fold in bread crumbs and Parmesan cheese. Place mixture in a 2 1/2-quart casserole dish that has been sprayed with cooking spray. Sprinkle top with extra bread crumbs and Parmesan cheese. Bake, covered, at 350° for 45 minutes; remove cover and bake for an additional 15 minutes.

Ste. Genevieve

Ste. Genevieve was Missouri's first permanent settlement having been founded by the French about 1735. The Church of Ste. Genevieve was built in 1876 and contains a 1663 religious painting. Visit historic homes and tour the museum to view American Indian relics, Civil War items, old coins and rare documents.

Homemade Noodles

"My grandmother and mother made these noodles; now I make them. They are a family favorite!"

Lola Coons—Down to Earth Lifestyles Bed & Breakfast, Parkville

1 EGG
SALT
FLOUR

In a mixing bowl, beat egg and season with salt to taste. Mix in enough flour to make the consistency of pie dough. Sprinkle flour onto a pastry cloth and place on a flat surface. Turn out dough onto cloth and roll until thin; allow to dry out, then cut into thin strips. Drop noodles into hot broth or prepared liquid and cook for 15-25 minutes or until tender.

Serves 1.

Mamaw Hancock's Piccalilli

"This was handed down from my husband's great-grandmother, to grandmother, mother, then to me. They were pioneers from Kentucky and Tennessee who lived in the South Central Ozark Mountains in Missouri. This is the best piccalilli I've ever tasted!"

Mary Jo Hancock—Scott City

2 parts CABBAGE to 1 part GREEN TOMATOES
Fresh HOT PEPPERS or dried
MEXICAN HOT PEPPERS
SALT

Grind cabbage and green tomatoes together; add hot peppers and salt to taste and stir well. Pack in a washed and scalded large stone crock, pressing down each addition until covered in its own juice. Cover with large cabbage leaves and hold down using a plate with a weight (also washed and scalded) on it to hold it down. Cover crock with cloth. Allow to stand for 10-14 days; skim off top and discard. Pack and seal in hot, sterilized jars.

Lazy Day Sweet Pickles

"This is a very old recipe from my German grandmother. We always had big gardens and did lots of canning. These pickles are so crisp and good!"

Mary Jo Hancock—Scott City

Small CUCUMBERS
1 Tbsp. PICKLING SALT
1 Tbsp. ALUM (food grade only)
COLD CIDER or WHITE VINEGAR
Syrup:
   1 1/4 cups SUGAR
   1 cup WATER
   1 1/2 tsp. PICKLING SPICE

Wash cucumbers and pack into a sterilized quart jar. Add pickling salt and alum to jar. Fill jar with cold cider and seal. Allow to stand for 6-8 weeks. Open jar, pour off cider and cut pickles into strips, chunks or slices as desired. To make syrup: Boil sugar, water and pickling spice together. Add pickles and bring to a boil again; remove from heat and cool for 12 hours.

Makes 1 quart.

President Harry S. Truman

Born in Lamar in 1884, Truman became a U.S. Senator in 1934, Vice-President of the U.S. in 1944 and President in 1945 when Franklin D. Roosevelt died. He was elected President in 1948. The Harry S. Truman Birthplace State Historic Park commemorates this great American.

Freezing Sweet Corn

Lillian Weber—Jackson

1 gal. SWEET CORN, cut from cob   **1 cup SUGAR**
1 qt. WATER   **4 tsp. PICKLING SALT**

In a large soup pot, combine all ingredients; heat to simmering and cook for 7 minutes. Drain, allow to cool, then place in food storage bags to freeze. When ready to use, just reheat.

Homemade Sauerkraut

"This recipe has been passed down in our family from one generation to the next. German people brought it to Missouri in the early 1930s."

Nola Garner Adams—Fulton

5 lbs. CABBAGE
3 1/2 Tbsp. PICKLING SALT

Trim and wash cabbage. Cut into fourths and drain with sliced side down; remove cores. Thinly shred cabbage and sprinkle with salt; mix thoroughly by hand. Wash a stone crock with hot, soapy water, rinse well and scald. Pack cabbage firmly and evenly into crock using a potato masher to press down. Repeat shredding, salting and packing cabbage until crock is filled to within 5 inches from the top. Press firmly with potato masher to force enough juice up to cover cabbage when crock is filled; keep cabbage covered with juice. Cover top with 2-3 layers of clean white cheesecloth, tucking edges down against the inside of crock. Place a scalded, heavy plate that just fits inside the crock on top of the cabbage and weigh it down with a large fruit jar filled with water (or use a stone) that has been washed and scalded. The juice needs to come over the plate.

Fermenting will begin the day following the packing. It works faster at a high temperature but the sauerkraut is more likely to spoil. The best quality product is made at a temperature of 70°. Remove the film daily. Wash and scald the cover and cloth as often as necessary to remove mold and film. When bubbling stops (12-14 days) tap the crock gently; if no bubbles rise, fermentation has ended.

Pack cabbage into sterilized quart jars to within 1 inch of the top. Cover with juices from crock. If more juice is needed, add a weak brine of 1 1/2 tablespoons of salt to 1 quart of water. Set jars in a kettle of cold water (water should come up to shoulder of jars). Bring water slowly to a boil, then remove jars and wipe off rims. Add lids and process in boiling water bath for 30 minutes at 212°.

Almond Rice Pilaf

Missouri Rice Research and Merchandising Council—Malden

1 Tbsp. BUTTER or MARGARINE
3/4 cup chopped ONION
1/2 cup slivered ALMONDS
2 cups CHICKEN BROTH
2 cups uncooked INSTANT RICE

In a medium saucepan, melt butter and sauté onion and almonds until onion is translucent and almonds are lightly browned. Add broth and bring to a boil. Stir in rice and cover. Remove from heat and allow to stand for 5 minutes or until liquid is absorbed.

Serves 6.

Fresh Missouri Peaches

Contact the Missouri Department of Agriculture's Market Development Division at 1-888-MO-BRAND for several free publications or for more information on locating fresh Missouri peaches.

Peach Seed Jelly

"This is an old and very good recipe."

Evelyn Hampton–Hampton's Greenhouse & Pumpkin Patch, Marshfield

Save all **PEACH SEEDS** when canning peaches. Cover seeds with **BOILING WATER** and let simmer on low for 5 minutes. Let stand overnight. Strain juice through a cloth. Measure **3 cups JUICE**, add **1 pkg. PECTIN** and bring to a vigorous boil. Add **3 cups SUGAR** and cook at boiling stage. As mixture nears jellying point, it will drop from the side of a spoon in two drops. When drops run together and slide off in a flake or sheet from the side of the spoon, the jelly is finished and should be removed from heat at once. Remove foam from jelly and pour into sterilized jelly glasses to within 1/4 inch from top and seal.

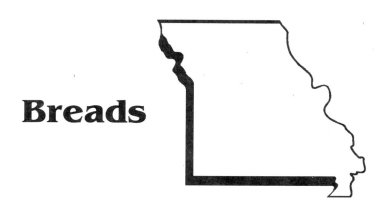

Breads

Hodgson Mill Yeast Muffins

Robert Weishaar—Hodgson Mill, Inc., Gainesville

1 pkg. (5/16 oz.) HODGSON MILL® REGULAR YEAST
2 cups WARM WATER
1/2 cup MARGARINE, melted
1/4 cup SUGAR
1 EGG, beaten
4 cups HODGSON MILL®
    UNBLEACHED FLOUR
1 Tbsp. BAKING POWDER
1 tsp. BAKING SODA

In a small bowl, dissolve yeast in warm water. In a large bowl, combine margarine and sugar; add egg and mix well. Stir in yeast mixture, flour, baking powder and baking soda and mix well. Batter can be stored in refrigerator in an airtight container. When ready to bake, stir batter down and spoon into greased or lined muffin tins until 2/3 full. Bake at 350° for 20 minutes or until golden brown.

Makes 2 dozen muffins.

Hodgson Mill Dinner Rolls

Robert Weishaar—Hodgson Mill, Inc., Gainesville

1 pkg. (5/16 oz.) HODGSON MILL® REGULAR YEAST
1 cup WARM WATER
1 cup MILK
1/4 cup SUGAR
2 tsp. SALT
1/4 cup SHORTENING
4 cups HODGSON MILL® UNBLEACHED
    FLOUR, divided
1 EGG

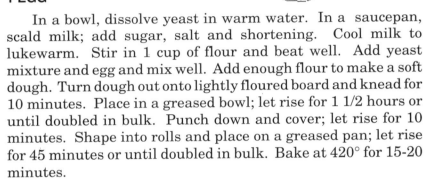

In a bowl, dissolve yeast in warm water. In a saucepan, scald milk; add sugar, salt and shortening. Cool milk to lukewarm. Stir in 1 cup of flour and beat well. Add yeast mixture and egg and mix well. Add enough flour to make a soft dough. Turn dough out onto lightly floured board and knead for 10 minutes. Place in a greased bowl; let rise for 1 1/2 hours or until doubled in bulk. Punch down and cover; let rise for 10 minutes. Shape into rolls and place on a greased pan; let rise for 45 minutes or until doubled in bulk. Bake at 420° for 15-20 minutes.

Makes 36-42 rolls.

Bran Loaf

"This recipe was found in Edwin Kraemer's home remedy book dated 1908. He is my husband's father."

Lillie Kraemer—Jackson

2 cups MILK
2 cups FLOUR
2 tsp. BAKING POWDER
2 Tbsp. BUTTER

4 cups BRAN
1 cup MOLASSES
2 tsp. SALT

In a large bowl, combine all ingredients and mix well. Pour batter into a greased loaf pan. Bake at 350° for 20 minutes or until toothpick inserted in center comes out clean.

Rye Bread

"This recipe won 'Best of Show' at the 1995 SEMO (Southeast Missouri) District Fair. I thought it would be fun to preserve it so I dried it and still have it displayed in a covered cake stand. It still looks good after all these years!"

Dortha J. Strack—Cape Girardeau

2 pkgs. (.25 oz. ea.) ACTIVE DRY YEAST
1 1/2 cups WARM WATER
3 Tbsp. SUGAR, divided
1/2 cup MOLASSES
1/4 cup HONEY
2 Tbsp. MARGARINE or SHORTENING, softened
2 tsp. SALT
Finely grated PEEL of 1 sm. ORANGE, optional
2 1/2 cups RYE FLOUR
2-3 cups WHITE BREAD FLOUR
CORNMEAL

In a large mixing bowl, dissolve yeast in warm water mixed with 1 tablespoon of sugar. Blend in molasses, honey, margarine, salt, remaining sugar and orange peel. Stir in rye flour and mix until smooth; add enough white flour to form a soft dough that is easy to handle. Turn dough out onto a floured surface and knead until smooth and elastic. Place dough in a greased bowl, turning so all sides are greased. Cover with a cloth and place in a warm, draft-free area to rise for 1-1 1/2 hours or until doubled in bulk. Return dough to floured surface, divide in half and shape into two round loaves. Place loaves on a lightly greased cookie sheet sprinkled with cornmeal. Cover with a warm, damp cloth; let rise for 1 hour. Preheat oven to 375°. Bake for 30-40 minutes or until golden brown.

Makes 2 loaves.

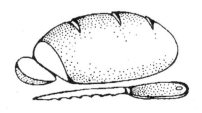

Angel Cornsticks

"This is my husband's favorite hot bread. I fix a pan of cornsticks 2 or 3 times a week."

Mrs. B.J. (Glenna) Garber—Carthage

1 1/2 cups CORNMEAL
1 cup FLOUR
1 1/2 tsp. BAKING POWDER
1/2 tsp. BAKING SODA
1 Tbsp. SUGAR
1 pkg. (.25 oz.) ACTIVE DRY YEAST

1/2 tsp. SALT
2 EGGS, beaten
2 cups NON-FAT
    BUTTERMILK
1/2 cup OIL

In a large bowl, combine dry ingredients. In a separate bowl, combine eggs, buttermilk and oil; stir into dry ingredients and mix well. Spoon batter into cornstick pans that have been sprayed with cooking spray. Bake at 450° for 12-15 minutes.

Makes 36 cornsticks.

Corn Muffins with a Kick

"Cornbread has always been a staple bread in our family through the generations, served with ham and beans, fried fish or rib dinners. Most of us do not have the time to make cornbread from scratch so we use our favorite mixes. Adding A Taste of the Kingdom® pepper jellies, products made by our family using produce from our farms, transforms standard cornbread into a gourmet treat with a kick!"

Julie Jones Price—A Taste of the Kingdom, LLC, Kingdom City

1 pkg. (16 oz.) CORNBREAD MUFFIN MIX
1 Tbsp. (heaping) A TASTE OF THE KINGDOM® PEPPER JELLY*

Prepare cornbread mix according to package directions. Soften pepper jelly by heating for 30 seconds in the microwave. Add pepper jelly to cornbread mixture and stir well. Bake as directed.

*Choose heat level as desired.

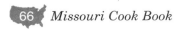

Victorian Veranda Cheese Danish Crescents

"This dish is a favorite with my guests. The recipe came from my aunt. She and her husband owned a small restaurant where they served a variety of creations to their family and customers."

Karen Forney—Victorian Veranda Bed & Breakfast, Bonne Terre

Dough:
- 2 1/2 cups FLOUR
- 1 tsp. BAKING POWDER
- 1 cup BUTTER or MARGARINE, cold
- 1/2 cup MILK
- 1 EGG, beaten

Filling:
- 1 pkg. (8 oz.) CREAM CHEESE, softened
- 1 EGG
- 1 Tbsp. LEMON JUICE
- 1/2 cup SUGAR
- 1 Tbsp. FLOUR

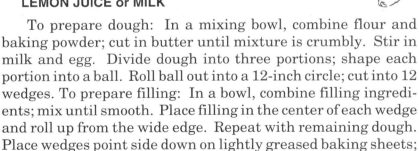

Glaze:
- 1 cup POWDERED SUGAR
- LEMON JUICE or MILK

To prepare dough: In a mixing bowl, combine flour and baking powder; cut in butter until mixture is crumbly. Stir in milk and egg. Divide dough into three portions; shape each portion into a ball. Roll ball out into a 12-inch circle; cut into 12 wedges. To prepare filling: In a bowl, combine filling ingredients; mix until smooth. Place filling in the center of each wedge and roll up from the wide edge. Repeat with remaining dough. Place wedges point side down on lightly greased baking sheets; form into crescent shapes. Bake at 350° for 16-18 minutes. To prepare glaze: Combine powdered sugar and enough lemon juice to form a thin glaze. Drizzle over tops of hot crescents.

Makes 36 crescents.

Pecan Muffins

"I found this recipe several years ago. I have revised it to use our Hodgson Mill® Insta-Bake, which is a product that is milled in Gainesville, 11 miles from our Bed & Breakfast."

Mary Morrison—Zanoni Mill Inn Bed & Breakfast, Zanoni

**2 cups HODGSON MILL®
INSTA-BAKE
2/3 cup MILK
1 tsp. VANILLA
1 tsp. CINNAMON**

**1/2 cup chopped PECANS
1/2 cup packed BROWN
SUGAR
1/4 cup MARGARINE or
BUTTER, melted**

In a large mixing bowl, combine Insta-Bake, milk, vanilla and cinnamon together. Stir in pecans, brown sugar and margarine. Spoon batter into lined muffin cups filling to 2/3 full. Bake at 350° for 15 minutes.

Makes 12 muffins.

Banana Bread

Wheat Foods Council—Columbia

**1/2 cup MARGARINE, softened
1 1/4 cups SUGAR
2 EGGS
1/2 cup LIGHT SOUR CREAM
1 cup mashed ripe BANANAS**

**1 tsp. BAKING SODA
2 cups FLOUR
1/4 cup MINI CHOCOLATE
CHIPS, optional**

Preheat oven to 350°. In a large bowl, cream margarine and sugar together with an electric mixer. Add eggs and beat until blended. Stir in sour cream and bananas and blend well. In a separate bowl, combine baking soda and flour; add to creamed mixture and beat on low until just mixed. Stir in chocolate chips. Pour batter into a 9 x 4 loaf pan that has been sprayed with cooking spray or greased and floured. Bake for 50-60 minutes or until toothpick inserted in center comes out clean. Let cool in pan for 5 minutes; remove and cool completely on wire rack.

Apple-Pumpkin Streusel Muffins

Missouri State Horticultural Society—Columbia

2 1/2 cups FLOUR
1 1/2 cups SUGAR
1 Tbsp. PUMPKIN PIE SPICE (or combine: cinnamon, nutmeg and
    a dash of cloves)
1/4 cup packed BROWN SUGAR
1/2 tsp. SALT
1 EGG, lightly beaten
1 cup canned PUMPKIN
1/2 cup VEGETABLE OIL
    or melted MARGARINE
2 cups finely chopped
    peeled fresh APPLES

Topping:
    2 Tbsp. FLOUR
    1/4 cup SUGAR
    1/2 tsp. CINNAMON
    4 tsp. BUTTER or MARGARINE

Preheat oven to 350°. In a mixing bowl, combine the first 5 ingredients; set aside. In a bowl, combine egg, pumpkin and oil. Add mixture to dry ingredients and stir until just moistened. Stir in apples. Spoon batter into greased or lined muffin cups, filling 3/4 full. To prepare topping: Combine flour, sugar and cinnamon; cut in butter until mixture is crumbly. Sprinkle topping over muffin batter. Bake for 30-40 minutes or until a toothpick inserted in the center comes out clean.

Jefferson City

This city was named after President Thomas Jefferson. Named Missouri's capital in 1826, the first capitol building was destroyed by fire in 1837. The second capitol building, completed in 1840, burned after being struck by lightning in 1911. The current structure was dedicated in 1924.

Low-Fat Cranberry Bread

Missouri Soybean Merchandising Council—Jefferson City

2 cups ALL-PURPOSE FLOUR
1/2 cup DEFATTED SOY FLOUR
3/4 cup SUGAR
2 Tbsp. POPPY SEEDS
1 Tbsp. BAKING POWDER
1/3 cup FAT-FREE SOY
    MARGARINE, melted

1 cup SKIM MILK
1/4 cup LIQUID EGG
    SUBSTITUTE
1 tsp. VANILLA
2 tsp. grated LEMON RIND
1 cup CRANBERRIES,
    chopped

Preheat oven to 350°. In a large bowl, combine flours, sugar, poppy seeds and baking powder. In another bowl, combine margarine, milk, egg, vanilla and lemon rind. Stir into flour mixture just until moistened. Stir in cranberries. Spoon batter into an 8 x 4 loaf pan which has been sprayed on the bottom with soy cooking spray. Bake for 60-70 minutes or until tests done. Cool in pan for 10 minutes, then remove and cool completely on a wire rack.

Calamity Jane

Born Martha Jane Canary in Princeton in 1852, Calamity Jane was a wandering frontierswoman who dressed like a man and frequented bars, telling stories of her adventures. She toured in Wild West shows and claimed to have been a Pony Express rider and a scout with General Custer's forces.

Corn Pone

3 Tbsp. LARD
3 cups CORNMEAL
2 1/2 cups BOILING WATER
3 tsp. SALT

Melt lard in a 10-inch cast iron skillet and swirl to coat. In a bowl, combine cornmeal, water and salt. Mix remaining fat from skillet into cornmeal mixture. Add batter to skillet and bake at 350° for 45-50 minutes or until golden brown.

Desserts

Blueberry Buckle

"After a morning of picking blueberries at a Missouri you-pick-it fruit farm, this makes a tasty treat."

Nancy Rezabek—Columbia

Batter:
3/4 cup SUGAR
1 stick MARGARINE
1 EGG, beaten
2 cups FLOUR

2 1/2 tsp. BAKING POWDER
1/2 cup MILK
2 cups fresh BLUEBERRIES

Topping:
1/2 cup SUGAR
1/2 cup FLOUR
1/2 tsp. CINNAMON
4 Tbsp. MARGARINE, softened

1/2 cup sliced ALMONDS

To prepare batter: In a large mixing bowl, combine sugar, margarine, egg, flour, baking powder and milk; mix well. Spread batter in a greased 13 x 9 baking pan; top with blueberries. To prepare topping: In a bowl, combine topping ingredients and mix well. Crumble topping over berries and sprinkle with almonds. Bake at 350° for 30-35 minutes or until a toothpick inserted in the center comes out clean.

My Valentine Special Tart

Kay Cameron—Cameron's Crag Bed & Breakfast, Branson

1/2 cup FLOUR
1/2 stick BUTTER

2 tsp. SUGAR

In a medium mixing bowl, combine flour, butter and sugar and blend well until mixture forms a smooth dough. Spread dough evenly into a thin, heart-shaped crust on a lightly greased baking sheet. Bake at 350° for 8-10 minutes until lightly browned; cool. Spread *Fruit Filling* over cooled crust and serve immediately before crust becomes soft.

Fruit Filling

4 oz. CREAM CHEESE
1/2 cup STRAWBERRY
  or RASPBERRY JAM

1/4 tsp. VANILLA
1/2 cup WHIPPED TOPPING
1/2 tsp. LEMON JUICE

In a small bowl, combine all ingredients together.

Baked Fudge

"This is an absolutely delicious recipe that is certain to please chocolate lovers."

Cathy McGeorge—Loganberry Inn Bed & Breakfast, Fulton

4 EGGS
2 cups SUGAR
1 cup BUTTER, melted

1/2 cup FLOUR
1/2 cup COCOA
2 tsp. VANILLA

Preheat oven to 325°. In a large bowl, cream eggs and sugar together; add butter. In a separate bowl, sift flour and cocoa together, then add to creamed mixture. Stir in vanilla. Pour into a greased 12 x 9 pan; set in a pan of hot water that reaches 1 inch on the side of the pan. Bake for 45-60 minutes or until top becomes crusty and inside stays soft. Serve warm with a scoop of ice cream.

Kolaches

"This recipe comes from an old family cookbook. The filling can be almost any kind of fruit—apple, cherry, peach, etc."

Leemer G. Cernohlavek—Red Bird Hill Apple Orchard, Fulton

Dough:
 3 pkgs. (.25 oz. ea.) ACTIVE DRY YEAST
 1/2 cup WARM WATER
 1 tsp. + 3/4 cup SUGAR, divided
 2 sticks BUTTER, softened
 3 EGG YOLKS
 3 tsp. SALT
 7 1/4 cups FLOUR, divided
 2 3/4 cups MILK, scalded and
 cooled to lukewarm

Apricot Filling:
 1 pkg. (10 oz.) dried APRICOTS
 1 1/2-2 cups SUGAR

Topping:
 1 cup SUGAR
 1/2 cup FLOUR
 1/2 tsp. CINNAMON
 2 Tbsp. BUTTER, melted

To prepare dough: In a tall glass, dissolve yeast in warm water and sprinkle in 1 teaspoon of sugar; set aside. In a mixer bowl, cream remaining sugar and butter together. Add egg yolks and salt and mix well. Stir in yeast mixture and 1 cup of flour and mix slowly with an electric mixer. Add milk and continue adding as much of the remaining flour as you can mix in with a wooden spoon. Knead in enough flour to form a soft dough. Continue kneading dough for 5 minutes until smooth and elastic. Shape dough into a ball and place in a lightly greased bowl, turning to grease the surface. Cover; let rise for 1-1 1/2 hours or until doubled in bulk. Punch down and turn dough out onto a lightly floured surface. Pinch off egg-size portions and roll each into a ball, using the palms of your hands.

(Continued next page)

Kolaches (continued)

Place balls approximately 1 inch apart on greased cookie sheets and brush tops with melted butter. Cover with a cloth; let rise for 1 hour. While kolaches are rising, prepare filling and topping. To prepare filling: Place apricots in a saucepan and cover with water. Cook slowly until fruit is soft and water has been cooked down; mash with a potato masher. Stir in sugar. Cook, uncovered, on low heat for 3-5 minutes, stirring constantly; allow to cool. To prepare topping: Combine all ingredients and stir until mixture resembles a coarse meal. With your fingers, make an indentation in each kolache and fill with 1 tablespoon of apricot filling. Sprinkle each with topping; let rise for 20 minutes. Bake at 425° for 10-15 minutes. Brush kolaches with butter immediately after removing from oven.

Makes 12 dozen kolaches.

Jelly Roll

"This is a delicious old-fashioned treat."

Robert Weishaar—Hodgson Mill, Inc., Gainesville

2 cups HODGSON MILL® UNBLEACHED FLOUR
2/3 cup SUGAR
1/2 tsp. BAKING POWDER
3/4 cup BUTTER, softened
1 EGG
1 tsp. VANILLA
1/3 cup STRAWBERRY, RASPBERRY or CHERRY JELLY or JAM

In a mixing bowl, combine flour, sugar and baking powder. Blend in butter, egg and vanilla. Divide dough into 4 parts and shape each part into a roll that is 1 inch in diameter. Place rolls 4 inches apart on an ungreased baking sheet. With the handle of a wooden spoon, make a 1/2-inch deep indentation down the center of each roll and fill with jelly. Bake at 350° for 20 minutes or until golden brown. Lift carefully onto cutting board and cut crosswise into bars 1-inch long. Cool on wire racks.

Makes 3 1/2 dozen 1-inch bars.

Fried Peach Peel Pie

"This was handed down by old timers that had seen hard times and learned not to waste anything!"

Evelyn Hampton–Hampton's Greenhouse & Pumpkin Patch, Marshfield

Take **one jar (quart or pint) canned or fresh PEACH PEELINGS** and add **1 cup SUGAR** with each **2 cups PEELINGS and JUICE.** Place in a saucepan and cook down until thick. Using your favorite **PIE CRUST,** cut out 6-inch circles. Put **2 tablespoons cooked PEACH PEELINGS** in center of each circle. Moisten edges of circles with **WATER** and fold over. Using a fork dipped in **FLOUR,** press around edges to seal.

In a 10-inch skillet, heat **2 tablespoons OIL or SHORTENING** and fry pies until golden brown, turn over and brown the other side.

Warsaw—A Town of Extremes!

Warsaw holds the state record for lowest temperature (-40°) on February 13, 1905 and also for the highest temperature recorded, (118°) on July 14, 1954.

Cracker Pecan Pie

Carol J. Bierschwal—Cape Girardeau

3 EGG WHITES, room temperature
1 cup SUGAR
1/2 tsp. BAKING SODA
3/4 cup crushed SODA CRACKERS
1 cup chopped PECANS
1 ctn. (8 oz.) COOL WHIP®

In a mixing bowl, beat egg whites until stiff. Gradually add sugar and baking soda; fold in crackers and 3/4 cup of pecans. Spoon mixture into a greased 9-inch round pan. Bake at 325° for 30 minutes; allow to cool. Spread Cool Whip on top and sprinkle with remaining pecans. Chill before serving.

Serves 6.

Nola's Fruitcake

"I love fruitcake, but do not like the alcohol most people soak them with. So, I got busy and came up with a recipe of my own. The carrots make this fruitcake moist. I make mini-loaves during the Christmas season and give them as gifts."

Nola Garner Adams—Fulton

8 oz. DATES, chopped
2 lb. MIXED CANDIED FRUIT
8 oz. CANDIED CHERRIES, chopped
4 oz. CANDIED PINEAPPLE, chopped
1 lb. PECANS, chopped
1 cup grated CARROTS
3 cups FLOUR
1 tsp. grated LEMON PEEL

1 tsp. BAKING POWDER
2 tsp. CINNAMON
1/2 tsp. NUTMEG
1 cup BUTTER or MARGARINE, softened
1/2 cup packed BROWN SUGAR
4 EGGS, lightly beaten
1 cup SUGAR
1/4 cup LIGHT KARO® SYRUP
1/4 cup ORANGE JUICE

In a large mixing bowl, combine dates, candied fruit, pecans and carrots and mix well; set aside. In a separate bowl, combine flour, lemon peel, baking powder, cinnamon and nutmeg and mix well. Pour over the candied fruit mixture and mix until all pieces are covered. In another bowl, beat butter, brown sugar, eggs, sugar, Karo syrup and orange juice together until smooth and creamy. Pour mixture over floured fruit and stir until fruit is well-covered. Spoon batter into 2 buttered loaf pans. Bake at 275° for 2 hours or until a toothpick inserted in the center comes out clean. Wrap loaves in plastic or foil, but do not refrigerate for several days so they will become moist.

Note: For 5 mini-loaf pans, cook at 350° for 30 minutes.

Lexington Monument

The "Madonna of the Trail" monument in Lexington tells the story of the brave women who helped conquer the West and is one of 12 placed in every state crossed by the National Old Trails road, the route of early settlers from Maryland to California.

Mom's Pineapple Upside-Down Cake

"This is my mother's recipe, which was passed down to her by her mother. I believe the original recipe came from a friend of Granny's who lived on a farm. This is the most flavorful lip-smacking upside-down cake you will ever treat your taste buds to and it's fast and easy to prepare. The smell of this cake baking and its flavor will take you back to your childhood."

Lawrence A. Stevens—The Dickey House Bed & Breakfast Ltd.,
Marshfield

1 stick BUTTER
1 cup packed BROWN SUGAR
1 can (20 oz.) sliced PINEAPPLE
1 jar (6 oz.) MARASCHINO CHERRIES
1/2-3/4 cup WALNUT HALVES
3 EGGS, separated
1 cup SUGAR
1 cup FLOUR
1 tsp. BAKING POWDER

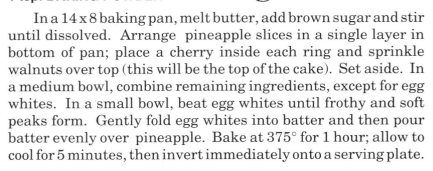

In a 14 x 8 baking pan, melt butter, add brown sugar and stir until dissolved. Arrange pineapple slices in a single layer in bottom of pan; place a cherry inside each ring and sprinkle walnuts over top (this will be the top of the cake). Set aside. In a medium bowl, combine remaining ingredients, except for egg whites. In a small bowl, beat egg whites until frothy and soft peaks form. Gently fold egg whites into batter and then pour batter evenly over pineapple. Bake at 375° for 1 hour; allow to cool for 5 minutes, then invert immediately onto a serving plate.

Did You Know?

The ice cream cone was invented at the St. Louis World's Fair in 1904 when an ice cream vendor ran out of cups and asked a waffle vendor to help by rolling up waffles to hold ice cream!

Grandma Moorhouse's Raisin Tarts

"My wife's great-grandmother was from England and always made these for the holidays. My mother-in-law recently redis-covered this recipe and passed it on to my wife."

Lawrence A. Stevens—The Dickey House Bed & Breakfast Ltd., Marshfield

1 (9-inch) unbaked PIE SHELL	1 tsp. VANILLA
3/4 cup RAISINS	1 EGG, beaten
3/4 cup packed BROWN SUGAR	1 Tbsp. BUTTER, melted
	POWDERED SUGAR

Roll out pie dough to 1/4-inch thickness and cut out 3-inch diameter circles. Press dough circles firmly into mini-muffin pan. Add raisins to each cup. In a medium mixing bowl, combine remaining ingredients, except powdered sugar and mix well. Place 1/2-1 teaspoon of batter on top of raisins in each cup. Bake at 350° for 12-14 minutes; allow to cool. Sprinkle with powdered sugar just before serving.

Sugar Cream Pie

"This is a family recipe. I grew up on a farm in Callaway County where we milked cows and had lots of cream, milk and butter. This was my dad's favorite pie."

Lola Coons—Down to Earth Lifestyles Bed & Breakfast, Parkville

Filling:

1 cup SUGAR	4 Tbsp. BUTTER
1 cup CREAM	3 Tbsp. CORNSTARCH
1 cup MILK	1/4 tsp. VANILLA

1 (9-inch) baked PIE SHELL
1 tsp. CINNAMON

In a large saucepan, combine sugar, cream, milk, butter and cornstarch and mix well. Cook over low heat until mixture thickens, then add vanilla. Pour filling into pie shell and sprinkle cinnamon on top. Chill before serving.

Old-Fashioned Tea Cakes

"I've been making these tea cakes for fifteen years.
They are wonderful!"

Pam Whyte—Prosperity School Bed & Breakfast, Joplin

1/2 cup SHORTENING	1 tsp. VANILLA
1/2 cup BUTTER	3 cups FLOUR
2 cups SUGAR	1 tsp. BAKING POWDER
2 EGGS	1 tsp. BAKING SODA
2 Tbsp. SOUR CREAM or	1 tsp. SALT
SOUR MILK	

In a large mixing bowl, cream shortening and butter together. Add sugar and beat until light and fluffy. Beat in eggs, one at a time. Stir in sour cream and vanilla and mix well. In a separate bowl, mix flour, baking powder, baking soda and salt. Combine with creamed mixture and mix thoroughly. Form dough into 1/2-inch balls and roll in sugar to coat. Place on a cookie sheet 2 inches apart and flatten with a glass that has been dipped in sugar. Bake at 375° for 8 minutes.

Branson
There are more theater seats in Branson than
there are on Broadway in New York City!

Poor Man's Biscuit Pie

"My maternal grandmother made this pie
often during the Depression."

Carol J. Bierschwal—Cape Girardeau

2 stale BISCUITS	1 1/2 cups MILK
1 (9-inch) unbaked PIE SHELL	1 tsp. VANILLA
1/2 cup SUGAR	1 EGG, lightly beaten
Dash of CINNAMON	

Crumble biscuits into pie shell; sprinkle with sugar and cinnamon. In a small mixing bowl, combine milk and vanilla; add egg and blend. Pour mixture over biscuits. Bake at 375° for 30 minutes or until set.

Strawberry Pizza

"A neighbor gave me this recipe several years ago when we first started growing and selling strawberries. It quickly became a family favorite."

Jo Ann Blackwell—Blackwell Family Produce, Salem

Crust:
 1 1/2 cups FLOUR
 1 cup MARGARINE, softened
 1/4 cup packed BROWN SUGAR
 2 cups chopped PECANS (optional)

Filling:
 1 pkg. (8 oz.) CREAM CHEESE, softened
 3/4 cup POWDERED SUGAR
 1 ctn. (8 oz.) COOL WHIP®

To prepare crust: In a mixing bowl, combine flour, margarine, brown sugar and pecans and mix with a pastry blender. Spread mixture onto a pizza pan or cookie sheet. Bake at 400° for 10-15 minutes; allow to cool. To prepare filling: In a bowl, blend cream cheese and powdered sugar together; fold in Cool Whip and spread over crust. Spread ***Strawberry Topping*** on top of filling. Chill before serving.

Strawberry Topping

 1 pkg. (3 oz.) STRAWBERRY JELL-O®
 1/2 cup SUGAR
 Dash of SALT
 1 cup WATER, divided
 4 Tbsp. CORNSTARCH
 4 cups sliced fresh or frozen STRAWBERRIES

In a saucepan, combine Jell-O, sugar, salt and 1/2 cup of water. In a bowl, dissolve cornstarch in remaining water and stir into Jell-O mixture. Cook over medium heat until thickened; remove from heat. Add strawberries and gently stir to coat. Allow mixture to cool.

Easy Spice Cake

"I have made this cake since 1955, the year my son Ed was born. I always make it for Thanksgiving and Christmas dinner. Everyone likes it and it is very easy to make."

Verona L. Wilder—Marble Hill

1 box (18.25 oz.) SPICE CAKE MIX
1 pint WHIPPING CREAM
3-4 ripe BANANAS, sliced
LEMON JUICE

Prepare cake mix according to package directions. Bake as directed using two 9-inch round pans. Allow cake layers to cool. In a mixing bowl, beat whipping cream until stiff. Spread 1/2 of the whipped cream on bottom cake layer. Dip banana slices in lemon juice and arrange on top of whipped cream. Place second cake layer on top, arrange remaining bananas on top and spread with remaining whipped cream.

Note: Cake can be made the day before and kept in a covered cake container. Add whipped cream and bananas an hour or two before serving to prevent bananas from turning brown.

Sawdust Pie

"This recipe is from my mother's friend. I guess with all the sawmills here they thought there ought to be a pie named for them!"

Martha M. Darrough—Farmington

Filling:
    7 EGG WHITES, unbeaten
    1 1/2 cups GRAHAM CRACKER CRUMBS
    1 1/2 cups SUGAR
    1 1/2 cups SHREDDED COCONUT
    1 1/2 cups PECANS
1 (9-inch) unbaked PIE SHELL

In a large bowl, combine all filling ingredients and mix well. Pour filling into pie shell and bake at 325° for 25 minutes.

Pumpkin Bars

"These are a delicious treat!"

Lillian Weber—Jackson

4 EGGS	1 tsp. BAKING SODA
1 2/3 cups SUGAR	2 tsp. BAKING POWDER
1 cup OIL	1/2 tsp. CINNAMON
2 cups FLOUR	2 cups PUMPKIN
1 tsp. SALT	1 tsp. VANILLA

In a bowl, beat together eggs, sugar and oil until light and fluffy. In another bowl, combine dry ingredients. Stir into egg mixture. Add pumpkin and vanilla and mix well. Spread batter into a greased and floured jelly roll pan and bake at 350° for 25-30 minutes. Let cool then cut into bars.

St. Joseph

Home to the Pony Express National Memorial commemorating that famous 1860 venture. This city was also the home of Jesse James, known then as Mr. Howard, prior to his assassination in 1882 by a fellow gang member for a $10,000 reward.

Hickory Nut Cookies

Lillie Kraemer—Jackson

1 cup SUGAR	1 1/2 tsp. BAKING SODA
1 cup packed BROWN SUGAR	1/2 tsp. SALT
1 cup MARGARINE or BUTTER	1 1/2 tsp. VANILLA
2 EGGS, beaten	2 cups HICKORY NUTS
4 cups FLOUR	

In a large mixing bowl, cream sugar, brown sugar and margarine together; add eggs and mix well. Stir in remaining ingredients and blend. Roll dough into 2-inch rolls. Slice dough into 1/4-inch slices, place on a lightly greased cookie sheet and bake at 350° for 5-10 minutes or until golden brown. Dough may be rolled in wax paper and frozen for later use.

1850 Blackberry Pie

Camden County Historical Society—Linn Creek

1 (10-inch) unbaked PIE SHELL
1 qt. fresh BLACKBERRIES
1 cup FLOUR

2 cups SUGAR
1 cup MILK

Fill pie shell with blackberries. In a mixing bowl, combine flour, sugar and milk and mix well. Pour mixture over berries. Bake at 350° for 45 minutes until center is set. Brown top by placing under broiler unit for a few minutes.

Cow Patties

Camden County Historical Society—Linn Creek

2 cups MILK CHOCOLATE CHIPS
1 Tbsp. SHORTENING

1/2 cup slivered ALMONDS
1/2 cup RAISINS

In a double boiler, melt chocolate chips and shortening over simmering water, stirring until smooth. Remove from heat; stir in almonds and raisins. Drop by tablespoons onto wax paper. Chill until ready to serve.

Makes 24 pieces.

Wedding Mints

Camden County Historical Society—Linn Creek

2 oz. CREAM CHEESE, softened
1 2/3 cups POWDERED SUGAR
SUGAR

In a medium mixing bowl, mix cream cheese and powdered sugar; shape into bite-size balls. Roll balls in sugar to coat. These can be pressed into molds after coating with sugar. Lay on wax paper until dry.

Note: Flavoring and coloring may be added to mixture.

Maple Walnut Brittle

Camden County Historical Society—Linn Creek

1 cup packed BROWN SUGAR
1 cup SUGAR
1/2 cup WATER
1/2 cup DARK CORN SYRUP
1/4 cup BUTTER
1 1/2 cups WALNUT PIECES
1/2 tsp. MAPLE FLAVORING

Butter a cookie sheet. In a medium saucepan, combine brown sugar, sugar, water and corn syrup and cook over medium heat until sugar dissolves. Bring mixture to a boil, stirring constantly. Continue cooking, without stirring, until candy thermometer reaches 300°. Remove syrup mixture from heat; stir in butter, nuts and flavoring. Quickly pour onto prepared cookie sheet and spread thin with a buttered spatula. Allow to cool and break into pieces. Store in an airtight container with wax paper between layers.

Pioneer Candy

Camden County Historical Society—Linn Creek

1 cup WARM UNSEASONED MASHED POTATOES
1/2 tsp. SALT
2 tsp. VANILLA
2 boxes (16 oz. ea.) POWDERED SUGAR
1 bag (12 oz.) SEMI-SWEET CHOCOLATE CHIPS, melted
NUTS or SHREDDED COCONUT

In a large bowl, mix potatoes, salt and vanilla together. Sift powdered sugar and add to mixture 1 cup at a time. Potatoes will liquefy at the first addition of powdered sugar and begin to thicken as more is added. When it reaches the consistency of a stiff dough, stop adding sugar and knead until smooth. Cover and chill until dough can be shaped into 1/2-inch balls. Dip in melted chocolate and roll in nuts or coconut.

Grandma B's Coconut Cream Pie

Jane Eckert—Eckert Family Farms, University City

Filling:
2 1/2 cups WHOLE MILK
3/4 cup SUGAR
2 Tbsp. FLOUR
2 1/2 Tbsp. CORNSTARCH

1/4 tsp. SALT
2 EGGS YOLKS, lightly
   beaten
1 tsp. VANILLA

Meringue:
4 EGG WHITES
4 Tbsp. SUGAR

1 (9-inch) baked PIE SHELL
1/2 cup COCONUT FLAKES

To prepare filling: Reserve 2 tablespoons of milk; set aside. Pour remaining milk into top of double boiler and bring to a boil. In a small bowl, combine reserved milk, sugar, flour, cornstarch and salt and mix well. Add egg yolks and stir until smooth. While milk is still boiling, add egg mixture and stir to thicken; remove from heat and stir in vanilla. To prepare meringue: In a mixing bowl, beat egg whites until stiff; add sugar, one tablespoon at a time and continue to beat until peaks form. Pour filling into pie shell; add coconut to filling, stirring gently. Spread meringue on top. Bake at 325° for 20 minutes or until meringue is golden.

The Ozarks

This mountain range stretches across southern Missouri, rising from the Ozark Plateau and is one of the oldest mountain ranges in North America. More than 4,000 caves and 60 springs can be found in this area. Big Spring near Van Buren, is the largest spring in the nation.

"Happy" Apple Cake

University of Missouri Department of Horticulture—Columbia

3 med. APPLES
1/4 cup packed BROWN
  SUGAR
1/4 cup BUTTER
2 tsp. CINNAMON
1 pkg. YELLOW CAKE MIX
1 1/4 cups WATER

1/4 cup OIL
1/3 cup BUTTER, softened
4 EGGS
1/4 cup QUICK OATS
1/2 cup GRAHAM CRACKER
  CRUMBS

Peel and chop apples, then place in a saucepan. Add brown sugar, 1/4 cup butter and cinnamon; cook until tender. Preheat oven to 350°. In a large mixing bowl, combine cake mix, water, oil, 1/3 cup butter, eggs, oats and graham cracker crumbs. Beat on low speed with electric mixer for 30 seconds, scraping bowl frequently. Fold in apples. Pour mixture into a greased and floured 13 x 9 pan; sprinkle with *Caramel Crunch Topping*. Bake 38-40 minutes or until cake pulls away from sides of pan and toothpick inserted in center comes out clean. Cool completely before serving.

Caramel Crunch Topping

1 cup GRAHAM CRACKER CRUMBS   1/4 cup packed BROWN
1/3 cup MELTED BUTTER   SUGAR

In a small bowl, combine all ingredients well.

Chipmunk Pie

Missouri Apple Merchandising Council—Columbia

3/4 cup SUGAR
1/2 cup FLOUR
1 tsp. BAKING POWDER
1 1/2 cups finely chopped,
  packed APPLES

1 EGG, beaten
1/2 cup chopped PECANS
1/2 tsp. CINNAMON
1 Tbsp. LEMON JUICE

Preheat oven to 350°. Combine all iungredients well and press into a greased 9 inch pie plate. Bake for 50-60 minutes.

Fresh Apple Cake

Missouri Apple Merchandising Council—Columbia

3 cups FLOUR
2 cups SUGAR
3 tsp. BAKING POWDER
Pinch of SALT
1 cup OIL
4 EGGS
2 tsp. VANILLA
1/2 cup ORANGE JUICE
1/2 cup SUGAR
1 tsp. CINNAMON
5 cups peeled thinly sliced APPLES

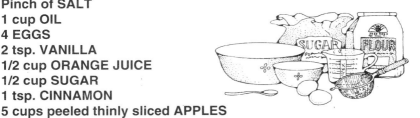

Preheat oven to 350°. In a large bowl, sift flour, sugar, baking powder and salt together. Add oil, eggs, vanilla and orange juice. Mix well. In another bowl, mix cinnamon and sugar together. Add apples to sugar mixture, stir to coat well. Grease and flour a 10-inch tube pan. Spoon and spread batter in pan, add a layer of apples. Add another layer of batter and apples, then a final layer of batter. Bake for one hour. Cool before serving.

Baked Apple Butter

Missouri Apple Merchandising Council—Columbia

6 lbs. APPLES   1/2 tsp. CINNAMON
SUGAR, as needed   1/2 tsp. ALLSPICE

Slice, peel and core apples. Put in a large kettle; add water until half the apples are covered. Cook over medium heat 15-20 minutes, or until softened; let cool. Preheat oven to 300°. Purée apples in blender or food processor. Measure purée. Add 1/2 cup sugar for each 1 cup of purée. Put purée mixture into a 13 x 9 glass baking dish. Stir in spices. Bake for 2-2 1/2 hours, or until butter is thick but not dry, stirring every 15 minutes. Ladle into clean, hot, sterilized jars, leaving 1/2 inch headspace. Process in boiling water bath for 10 minutes.

Yields 6 pints.

Missouri
Food Festival Sampler

April—Tulip Festival, Owensville. **World Fest**, Branson.

May—Mushroom Festival, Richmond. **ArtFair & WineFest**, Washington. **Cinco de Mayo**, Jefferson City. **Hillsboro Festival**, Hillsboro. **Kimmswick Days**, Kimmswick.

June—Salisbury Steak Festival, Salisbury. **BBQ Competition**, Raytown. **Renaissance Festival**, Sedalia. **Strawberry Festival**, Kimmswick. **Taste of Kimmswick**, Kimmswick. **Jubilee Days**, Warsaw.

July—Orrick Potato Festival, Orrick. **Missouri Wine Festival**, Osage Beach. **Sweet Corn Festival**, East Prairie. **Bolivar Country Days**, Bolivar. **St. Louis Fair**, St. Louis. **Sweet Springs Festival**, Sweet Springs.

August—Norborne Soybean Festival, Norborne. **Village of Laurie BBQ Cookoff**, Laurie. **Missouri Black Expo Food Festival**, St. Louis. **Texas County Fair**, Houston. **Dent County Fall Festival**, Salem.

September—Grape & Fall Festival, St. James. **Ozark Ham & Turkey Festival**, California. **Hillbilly Fair**, Laurie. **SEMO District Fair**, Cape Girardeau. **National Soybean Festival**, Portageville. **Missouri Fall Festival**, Columbia. **Heritage Day**, Houston. **Seymour Apple Festival**, Seymour. **Ozark Berry Festival**, Mt. Vernon. **Japan Festival**, Kansas City. **Arnold Days**, Arnold. **De Soto Fall Festival**, De Soto. **Slater Fall Festival**, Slater. **Wellington Fair**, Wellington.

October—Brunswick Pecan Festival, Brunswick. **Eldon Turkey Festival**, Eldon. **Olde Tyme Apple Festival**, Versailles. **Oktoberfest**, St. Joseph. **Pumpkinfest**, St. Joseph **AppleFest**, Weston. **Oktoberfest**, Kansas City. **Oktoberfest**, Hermann. **Apple Butter Festival**, Kimmswick. **Oktoberfest**, Augusta. **Oktoberfest**, St. Charles. **German Oktoberfest**, Rolla. **Deutsch Country Days**, Marthasville.

Index

Index (continued)

Index (continued)

Index (continued)

Recipe Contributors

Nola Garner Adams, Fulton 61, 76

Ronnie Alewel–Missouri Association of Meat Processors, Sedalia 46, 51

Ronnie Alewel, Sedalia 57

Carol J. Bierschwal, Cape Girardeau 75, 79

Jo Ann Blackwell–Blackwell Family Produce, Salem 56, 80

Cynthia Brogdon, The Doanleigh Inn, Supreme Bean, Kansas City 9, 13, 20, 39

Camden County Historical Society, Linn Creek 24, 83-84

Kay Cameron–Cameron's Crag Bed & Breakfast, Branson 16-17, 72

Leemer G. Cernohlavek–Red Bird Hill Apple Orchard, Fulton 73

Cheryl Compton–Compton Family Farm, Tunas 53-54

Lola Coons–Down to Earth Lifestyles Bed & Breakfast, Parkville 59, 78

Kathy & Tom' Corey–Rock Eddy Bluff Farm-A Country Retreat, Dixon 25, 30

Martha M. Darrough, Farmington 8, 55, 81

Jane Due–Ray Home Bed & Breakfast, Gallatin 21

Jane Eckert–Eckert Family Farms, University City 85

Karen Forney–Victorian Veranda Bed & Breakfast, Bonne Terre 44, 67

Mrs. B.J. Garber, Carthage 38, 52, 66

Betty Glastetter, Oran 22, 26

Goats-R-Us–United Missouri Goat Producers, Salem 11

Barbara Gray, Ballwin 10, 29

Robert A. Gray, Ballwin 19, 28

Greater Missouri Ostrich Assn., Hermitage 12

Dwain Hammons, Hammons Products Company, Stockton 34

Evelyn Hampton–Hampton's Greenhouse & Pumpkin Patch, Marshfield 62, 75

Mary Jo Hancock, Scott City 50, 59-60

Michael Hixson–Louis Maull Co., St. Louis 48

Lillie Kraemer, Jackson 46, 64, 82

Rhona Lococo—Lococo House II Bed & Breakfast, St. Charles 16

Debbie Mahaney–Shepherdsfield Country Store & Bakery, Fulton 23, 27

Cathy McGeorge–Loganberry Inn Bed & Breakfast, Fulton 22, 72

Julia K. McMillan, Kansas City 38

Margot McMillen–Timber Hill Farm, Fulton 40

Missouri Apple Merchandising Council, Columbia 33, 87

Missouri-Arkansas Watermelon Association, Kennett 33

Missouri Beef Industry Council, Columbia 36

Missouri Pork Producers Association, Columbia 32, 45

Missouri Rice Research & Merchandising Council, Malden 62

Missouri Small Fruit Growers Association, Neosho 31

Missouri Soybean Merchandising Council—Jefferson City 10, 12, 49, 51, 70

Missouri State Horticultural Society, Columbia 69, 86

Mary Morrison–Zanoni Mill Inn Bed & Breakfast, Zanoni 68

Lori & Dean Murray–Eastlake Inn Bed & Breakfast, St. Louis 17

Julie Jones Price–A Taste of the Kingdom, LLC, Kingdom City 11, 42, 66

Nancy Rauseo–Mariah Acres, Cameron 44

Nancy Rezabek, Columbia 43, 50, 71

Nancy Scott–Daddy Buck's Inc., Linn Creek 48

Georgia L. Snider, Chaffee 26, 43

Stan Squires–Halben Foods, St. Louis 47, 54

Lawrence A. Stevens–The Dickey House Bed & Breakfast Ltd., Marshfield 18, 77-78

Dortha J. Strack, Cape Girardeau 7, 57, 65

Carolyn & George Sweet–Sweetbriar Bed & Breakfast, Fayette 15

Thomas A. Tucker–Vivienne Dressings/ Tucker Food Products Inc., St. Louis 8, 31, 41

Lillian Weber, Jackson 60, 82

Robert Weishaar–Hodgson Mill, Inc., Gainesville 63-64, 74

Wheat Foods Council—Columbia 35, 68

Pam Whyte–Prosperity School Bed & Breakfast, Joplin 41, 79

Verona L. Wilder, Marble Hill 58, 81

IOWA COOK BOOK

Recipes from across America's heartland. From *Indian Two-Corn Pudding* to *Pork Chops Braised in White Wine* this cookbook presents home-grown favorites and encompasses both ethnic traditions and gourmet specialties. A special section, "Iowa Corn Recipes" highlights this state's most famous export.
5 1/2 x 8 1/2 — 96 pages . . . $6.95

ILLINOIS COOK BOOK

Enjoy the flavors of Illinois! Over 100 recipes that celebrate Illinois. *Reuben in the Round, Pork Medallions in Herb Sauce, Autumn's Swiss Supper, Carrot Soufflé, Sky High Honey Biscuits* and *Rhubarb Cream Pie*, to name just a few. Includes fascinating facts and trivia.
5 1/2 x 8 1/2 — 96 pages . . . $6.95

KANSAS COOK BOOK

Over 125 luscious recipes capture the rich cultural and histori-cal charm of Kansas. Traditional and contemporary recipes include favorites such as *Pumpkin Dumplin's with Apple Chutney, Sunflower Salad, Kansas Beef Strogonoff, Corn Fritters* and *Yellow Brick Road Cake*. Includes entertaining Kansas trivia and facts.
5 1/2 x 8 1/2 — 96 pages . . . $6.95

MINNESOTA COOK BOOK

Featuring Minnesota's rich blend of cultures and culinary traditions. Eye-opening breakfast and brunch selections, distinctive soup and salad recipes, savory main and side dishes and delicious desserts. From *Zucchini Pancakes* to *Swedish Almond Rusks,* you'll find recipes for every occasion!
5 1/2 x 8 1/2 — 96 pages . . . $6.95

OKLAHOMA COOK BOOK

From *Indian Fry Bread* to *Chicken Fried Steak* and from *Pineapple-Zucchini Bread* to *Shoo-fly Pie*, this cookbook presents homegrown recipes that encompass the many ethnic traditions that are part of this state's history. Enjoy these recipes as you learn the history and the unique down-home taste of Oklahoma cooking!
5 1/2 x 8 1/2 — 96 pages . . . $6.95

ORDER BLANK

GOLDEN WEST PUBLISHERS

☼ 4113 N. Longview Ave. • Phoenix, AZ 85014
www.goldenwestpublishers.com • **1-800-658-5830** • FAX 602-279-6901

Qty	Title	Price	Amount
	Apple Lovers Cook Book	6.95	
	Bean Lovers Cook Book	6.95	
	Berry Lovers Cook Book	6.95	
	Best Barbecue Recipes	6.95	
	Chili-Lovers' Cook Book	6.95	
	Corn Lovers Cook Book	6.95	
	Easy Recipes for Wild Game & Fish	6.95	
	Illinois Cook Book	6.95	
	Indiana Cook Book	6.95	
	Iowa Cook Book	6.95	
	Joy of Muffins	6.95	
	Kansas Cook Book	6.95	
	Kentucky Cook Book	6.95	
	Minnesota Cook Book	6.95	
	Missouri Cook Book	6.95	
	Oklahoma Cook Book	6.95	
	Pumpkin Lovers Cook Book	6.95	
	Recipes for a Healthy Lifestyle	6.95	
	Salsa Lovers Cook Book	6.95	
	Veggie Lovers Cook Book	6.95	
Shipping & Handling Add:	United States $4.00 Canada & Mexico $6.00—All others $13.00		

☐ My Check or Money Order Enclosed

☐ MasterCard ☐ VISA

Total $ _____

(Payable in U.S. funds)

Acct. No. _____ Exp. Date _____

Signature _____

Name _____ Phone _____

Address _____

City/State/Zip _____

Call for a FREE catalog of all of our titles

5/04   **This order blank may be photocopied**   Missouri